MW00451309

SCABS, SCARS, AND POTS O'GOLD

TRUE-LIFE STORIES OF A SUCCESSFUL FRANCHISEE

SCOTT B. WARD

United States, 2020

All rights reserved. No part of this book may be used or reproduced in any manner whatsoever without the written permission of the author and publisher. Printed in the United States of America.

Publisher information address: Scott B. Ward, 335 Junction Track, Roswell, GA 30075

www.scottbward.net

Cover art and design by Carolyn D. Ward

First Edition, 2020

Paperback ISBN: 978-1-73553668-0-7

Library of Congress Control Number: 2020912610

"Scott's perspective on Entrepreneurship brings it home! How many times as a business owner did I say "I got this, it can't be that hard"

Each chapter brings back memories and ideas of things I wish I had in my tool kit at the time! Scott you have a winner!"

Steve Stroud, Executive Director, Roswell, Inc.

"Scott Ward shares his inspiring story of lessons learned on his journey of being a 28-year multi-store retailer who successfully opened, operated, and then sold his business...which is no easy feat. Scabs, Scars, and Pots O' Gold, True-Life Stories of a Successful Franchisee is full of funny anecdotes and practical concepts which seamlessly tie back to business and the spirit of persevering through setbacks. Wish I would have had this when I was getting started, yet there are true nuggets of gold even for this 26-year retail veteran. If you really want to be a successful entrepreneur, consider carrying his playbook in your hip pocket."

Jay Crook, Owner, Play It Again Sports, Kennesaw, GA

CONTENTS

ACKNOWLEDGMENTS

All of these stories are relatable to so many business people I've worked with through the years. I want to thank them for pushing me to write these down in my own words. I give special props and kudos to Carolyn Ward, my artist and partner in life. Thanks also to author and consultant Ted Richardson, an awesome, giving person, who never said no to my questions.

INTRODUCTION

A business idea "hits like a thunderbolt"!

BEFORE I HAD to cover payroll with an advance on my personal credit card, before I had to fire a guy for making lewd comments to a female coworker only to find out later she had dropped the shared company phone in the toilet on purpose and put nails under people's tires for kicks, before I had half my money sucked out of my business checking account because a vendor had not been paid for two years but they were sending all the notifications to the wrong address, before one of my managers got scammed through an electric bill fraud, before opening way too many stores in too short a time, before I had to actually explain to an IRS agent "helping" me with back taxes how a balance sheet and profit and loss report work...

I looked out of the window of my corporate advertising office and saw the owner of the agency getting out of his nice car as he came in late. He had probably been working at home, but the luxury of taking care of things in his own time and in his own way seemed very appealing. That's when my brain first started whirring with the possibility of achieving the same for myself. And the questions started. How did he do it? How have others done it? How can I do it? He's not so special. For Pete's sake, if he can do it certainly I can! And the questions kept coming and pouring in and you tend to get overwhelmed because there are no pat answers. The phone rings, and the business at hand interrupts your dreams. The questions get put aside. A day, a month, years can go by.

But I really wanted it. I really craved the total responsibility. The diligence, curiosity, and persistence, like training in any discipline, made my mind aware and ready to see the right opportunity. That's what happened to me when I discovered Play It Again Sports. Thus began my path to becoming a franchisee small business owner and an integral part of my community. A small business path that led to economic stability, independence, and the strength to push as far as I could dream. My small business provided a home, vacations, and college educations for my family. I provided income for several hundred employees through the years. I mentored five employees to go on and become owners themselves. These examples are a few of my many pots of gold. But the biggest pot of gold and satisfaction was to successfully build an asset, then sell it! You don't even have to take my word for it. Talk to a local bank teller. They'll tell you most of the biggest deposits they see come from individuals who own their own businesses. But—

I was a customer first. I, like many people, drove past a store about eight times during my daily activities. And I was always curious until finally one day my curiosity got the better of me and I stopped. It was such a cool store filled with neat, clean, gently used, and new sports stuff. The owner's dog lay on the floor, and he gave everyone that little thump-thump tail wag without lifting his head. It had a good vibe. Now I wasn't looking to start a business at the time. I was just curious about it from a shopper's viewpoint. I conversed with the owner and bought a $29 set of golf irons. I also picked up the owner's card.

Later that year we relocated to a different city. My wife got a great full-time job, and I moved on to "freelancing." I thought it was a good time to explore starting my own business. My career was in the advertising and film production business, but this was 1991 and a huge recession was in progress. The airlines were caving after deregulation in the 1980s. IBM had laid off 50,000 cubicle occupants, and ad budgets were being slashed all over the country. Not a good time to open my own agency. But I thought of Play It Again Sports. Kids, recycling, community, and sports, and how those are things that will never go out of style, recession or no recession. There were no stores in my metro area so I decided I might as well see if I could do it. So I started by asking the basic questions to friends and family. "Hey, I'm thinking of opening a business; here's the concept. What do you think?" And the first responses I received from everyone were more questions. "What's your plan? What are your goals? How are you going to fund this business?"

All right, I now knew I needed a plan. I could do that! I've made plans before! I'll bet you have, too. Remember when you were a kid and you "hatched a plan" to steal your cousin's dolls and put GI Joe clothes on them, or you and your buddies were going to the woods behind your neighborhood and chop down real trees—REAL BIG TREES to build a real log cabin. Or as a fraternity brother you threw a slightly illegal party with a band, waterfall, and ankle-deep pool of water to dance in. You had to have a plan. So, I made my plan. That plan I created and executed gave me many years' worth of stories that all have a business message. I'm going to share some stories that will make you money!

This little book of personal stories is not meant to be a "how to" book. It's meant to remind you and encourage you to think about topics you might not have thought about. It's meant to bring up topics and uncomfortable results that can happen when you ignore topics you don't want to deal with. This book is meant to inspire you from that first thunderbolt idea to the moment you "slingshot" someone else forward to success, and then to the day you sell your asset.

I'm sharing these stories because after twenty-eight years of fun and craziness, collecting scabs, scars, and joy in the franchisee retail business, I wanted to share the pots o'gold. As a local entrepreneur and businessperson, I am an integral part of the community. I have developed so many great customers and friends. I also encountered so many rascals and smooth talkers.

I also participated on buying committees and the National Franchise Advisory Council for Winmark Corporation, where I was eventually elected chairman. I won the Ruth Cerrell Award for Lifetime Achievement, which is voted on by fellow franchisees and given by the franchisor in honor of Ruth Cerrell, an amazing store owner from Wisconsin who exemplified great business skills and a long-term giving, helping, spirit to the community and to the franchise. I joined local nonprofit boards, adding value to my community. As I was preparing to sell my last franchise, I was relating some of my stories to a customer who stopped me and said, "Scott, you've got to write this stuff down!" So here it is. I'm writing it down for you. It may not be as eloquent as Chaucer. Or as heroic as Hemingway. But I hope it brings a smile to your face. I hope you give the local business owners a bit of patience the next time you interact with one. And do frequent them often. I hope the lessons I learned, no matter your level of business experience, will help you to keep your scabs clean, your scars not as gruesome, and your pots of gold even more brilliant than mine! Believe me, if you go down the road of owning a small business or franchise, you will get scabs and scars aplenty. But pick yourself up. Dust yourself off. Keep your head on a swivel. Because you will also find many pots o' gold!

1

Is Small Business for You?

"But hey, I worked for IBM!"

IT SEEMS LIKE during every recession there is a gaggle of layoffs. The market is inundated with corporate mid-level managers from Fortune 500 companies that have received a parachute of money to get them the hell off the quarterly earnings cash flow statement. And franchisors love it. Why? Because franchises are a great place for middle-aged downsized business folks to get in a business and invest or start a second career. But be careful. The ego can erupt. Preconceived ideas about small business and franchising are booby traps. This chapter is going to give you some insights into good and bad reasons to go into business for yourself. You'll find tips on self-evaluation and evaluating a good franchise match. "But I watch CNBC, read the *Wall Street Journal*, and have a great portfolio," you might say. Yes, as a conqueror of the corporate arena, software cowboy, or engineering phenom you've acquired amazing acumen, but the many hats needed for face-to-face small business is another animal.

As a franchisee, I survived three recessions: 1991–1993, the mini tech-crash of 2000, and the Great Recession that began late 2007. Every single time there were franchisees that came into the system with this attitude: Mr. Downsized, "Well, I've run a division of IBM for twenty years with one hundred direct reports so I can run a sports store!" Mr. Techie, "If you would just put more into the point of sale system then I could cut back on employees, and I could do everything myself while just standing at the counter." The fact is, both of these people are right. They probably do have the skills to run their own business. But it's not a given.

I saw close to five hundred franchisees buy an existing store or start their own, then run them into the ground within three years. There was nothing wrong with the concept or the location of these businesses. The owners got hit with a reality check. Just because you like food doesn't mean you can be successful running an eatery. Just because you like sports doesn't mean you can operate a sporting goods store. Just because you are a "people person" doesn't mean you can run a business at all. If you've been über-successful in the corporate world are you ready for the maddening, crappy details of small business? If you and your family have never been in the circle of business owners, how do you know if you should risk it all and completely transform your lifestyle and routines?

"Oh, you mean I can't fund it, then hire a manager and go play golf three times a week?"

No. Just like any business, but especially a start-up, you better be prepared to eat it, sleep it, and drink it for years. For example, people who are successful with restaurants love people and serving food. Many will admit they would do it for no pay at all.

So, how do you know if you have the right stuff? Ask if you can shadow the owner or manager of the particular concept you are interested in buying and work there. And not just a few times a month during slow times. Work the weekends and holidays. Put in five days a week from open to close for a month if you can. Even if that open to close is 10 a.m. until 9 p.m. Like fresh rain on a patch of weeds, you will be amazed at what you see develop. Watch the interactions of employees and customers. Watch the interactions of employees with other employees. Become aware of your own interactions with customers. Experience how the employees respond to you. Watch how this changes with the time of day, workload, and full-timers vs. part-timers. Now here is the great Zen Buddhism part—become aware of your own interactions and feelings to all of the above. Is it motivating? Are you biting at the bit to get in and make recommendations? Training? Is there a little thrill in your heart when you see the potential of what you and your personal skill set can accomplish with this type of business? Is it good?

Now there are a gazillion different types of tests you could run on yourself. Job knowledge, skills, integrity, cognitive, personality, emotional, and physical. If you've been in corporate America you've been subjected to these. They are not a pass-fail type of test. They generally pull back the layers of personality and shine light on aspects of your strengths and weaknesses you knew or suspected about yourself all along. Being openly aware of your strengths and weaknesses is vital because you are about to start building a team around you for success.

(Hint—no one built their business by themselves. And this constant building never stops. Not even for one day.) By no means am I suggesting you use one of these tests to determine if you should buy a franchise or go into business for yourself. It is one small (and fun) part of gathering the data so you can make a confident and informed decision. I suggest doing one every five years or so just to see how you have changed. I like tests because I'm curious. I'm especially curious about what motivates people, especially me! So, here are a few used by businesses all over the world.

According to TopResume, the five most popular personality tests are:

1. The Caliper Profile offers guides to match personality to job performance. https://calipercorp.com/caliper-profile/
2. The Myers-Briggs Type Indicator identifies how your personality "leans." For example, "Thinking vs. Feeling":
   www.themyersbriggs.com.
3. The SHL Occupational Personality Questionnaire gives you an idea of how your behaviors might influence your work performance:
   www.shl.com.
4. The Hogan Personality Inventory test evaluates your temperament and how it matches the demands of a position:
   www.hoganassessments.com.
5. The DISC Behavior Inventory evaluation measures a person's four personality types. Those four are designated "Dominant (D)," "Influential (I)," "Steady (S)," and "Compliant":
   www.discprofile.com[1]

And none of us are all or nothing in any one of these, but we are this vast gray scale of emotion and motivation. You are starting to build a brand-new baby organization that could (and we hope) grow to whatever your dreams can imagine. It starts with you. Shouldn't you know as much as possible about that first building block—you—as possible? If you've been there, done that, then fine, but it never hurts to check under the hood once in a while. If you're new to this type of team-building evaluation, take at least one of these tests. It's fun! And you might as well use what the top companies in the world have used!

But none of those tests are as good as jumping in with both feet and just doing it for a time before you permanently transition. Now, after some self-examination and research on your business idea or franchise, what's the next step? Ask yourself, "Would I hire me?"

Highlights

No matter how intriguing, small business isn't for everyone.
1. Spend time working in the business (or a similar one) you want to own.
2. Take a professional personality test.

2

Franchisors

What good are they? Why do I need one?

HAVE YOU EVER purchased a "kit"? You know, a brand-new, complete experience all wrapped up in a nice easy box guaranteed to get you started: A bread-making kit. A beer-brewing kit. A fly-fishing kit. Heck, you can build airplanes and houses from a kit. Well, franchises are business kits that provide a quicker and easier way to get up and running. The franchise is supposed to provide everything you need to be successful in a particular enterprise; however, they cannot guarantee success. In this section I've included some stories about franchisee and franchisor relationships—issues to watch out for, questions to ask.

Perhaps you've chosen the business category you want to open, but there are a multitude of franchisors to choose from. Or should you start your own independent business without a franchisor? In general, it's an accepted fact that franchises have a higher survival rate than independent start-ups, but the percentages after two years and five years vary widely. GuidantFinancial.com states "franchise success rates even vary by industry" and according to them, "franchises in the financial, education, real estate, and health industries have a twenty percent better success rate than others."[1] Independent franchise consultants are very helpful at researching and matching you with a franchise that best fits your needs. Also, a franchise consultant is usually free to you because the franchisor pays them a finder's fee. Franchises should also provide economies of scale. Good franchises will provide discounts on expense items such as fixtures, credit card processing, property insurance, outside marketing vendors, shipping vendors, and signage. They should also provide basic financial training, marketing training, site selection, inventory and procurement, hiring and firing, legal issues pertaining to your particular industry, and insight into overall trends regionally and worldwide. Typically, it is also easier to sell a franchise business than an independent business because the buyer feels they have better structure and marketing visibility behind a franchise name.

These key business insights are much tougher to get as an independent. Franchisors ensure the cupcake-making, sign-making, pizza-selling, massage, home care, or gym business is going smoothly, and they provide an exit plan for the future.

You may be thinking, *Oh—you mean I'm not going to do this until I die?* When you sign "I do" and get hitched to a franchisor, you better plan for the divorce from the get-go. This is not love. This is building an asset.

Like many others, I grew up in an environment that didn't prepare me for a successful business career. My dad lived with me and my mom until I was thirteen, then a divorce carried him off. I was blessed to see him about three times a year after that. And no one in my family had ever owned their own business. In fact, only a few of my family members had graduated from college and not with business degrees. We lived paycheck to paycheck. The people, family, and friends we were around were the same. Most men in the family died before age fifty or ran off. This was back before many women owned businesses. I moved about sixteen times in my first eighteen years. My point is, people learn an awful lot by osmosis—ordinary family conversations around the kitchen table. If your family is immersed in business or farming or restaurants or retail, by age fourteen you may have picked up the knowledge to run that business. Have you ever read an article about an up-and-coming businessperson? Somewhere in the article that person will talk about their parent or grandfather or aunt setting an example and influencing them. It's a powerful baton to pass on. And that power is just as powerful in a negative sense when your example of how to manage a household budget is, "Well, there's money in the checkbook so we can spend it. Payday is just three days away." It's tough to run a business with that mindset.

So how do you know if your franchise-provided "kit" for business is going to be enough? Enough to get you started? Enough to support you when things go sideways? Enough to support you when you want to sell the asset you've built? The simple truth is, like all starter kits, franchises are a license to learn. Like that driver's license when you were sixteen. You have to pay attention and keep learning. Because eventually your business will hit an icy patch and just like a car it WILL go sideways. It could be with a vendor, a lease, forced upgrades, territory rights, and on and on. Does the franchisor have a dedicated person to guide you? How quickly do they respond and take action? Is there a freethinking franchisee council to represent you and your fellow franchisees? What is the franchisor's history? How many openings, closings, and resales? What are the trends?

A May 27, 2014, *Forbes* article lists thirteen mistakes new franchisees make. (I have a personal list of mistakes new franchisees make, which is even longer.) But let's focus on a few critical points: 1. "You should not buy a franchise to be your own boss or control your destiny." Everyone answers to someone and depending on the franchise you may have a longer leash than others, but you still operate within a system. That's the trade-off, but hopefully you will have a more valuable asset to sell because it is part of a reputable system. 2. You should not believe a franchise is a fail-safe. "Franchises actually fail at about the same rate as independent businesses." 3." Hire an experienced franchise attorney before signing" anything, much less the full agreement. 4. "Spend time in the business" and speak with owners of those businesses in other parts of the country.[2]

Another great comparison tool is the Federal Trade Commission's required Franchise Disclosure Document. All franchises are required to supply you with one. Compare this document to other franchise groups' disclosure documents. Maybe there's a franchise in an industry or price range you don't want to be in or can't afford but you really respect. Try to obtain the respected franchisor's disclosure document and compare it to the franchise you are considering. It probably will reveal questions to ask about support, training, and future growth strategies of the franchise. Once again, we go back to asking questions.

My particular franchise has had several different corporate owners. When we were interviewing the original franchisor and they us, this is how the inventory management process of a store was explained: The franchisor would provide a recommended first order of inventory. If something sells, buy more. If it sells well, buy a lot more. If it doesn't sell, don't buy more.

Eureka! Now, that is very reasonable and makes a lot of sense. It is basic Business Inventory 101. But the practical reality should have given us a warning flag. This franchisor didn't know much more than we did. And we didn't know squat! Other examples indicated our franchisor was inexperienced. The letters of credit we issued to the buying group for inventory, letters of credit proving we had the funds to pay our bills, were kept in a little plastic box behind the desk of the corporate head of the buying group. He was also running four of his own stores at the same time. This was all back when business was conducted by fax machine. There were no computers. We should have asked a few more questions.

The good news is that original franchisor was sincere in wanting us all to improve. They listened to feedback. They provided financial training and conferences with continuing education. So we learned at the same pace they did, but we had to stay active and engaged with the franchisor, too.

Did I say we had the same learning curve as the franchisor? Yes. The franchisor wasn't vetting prospective franchisees thoroughly. Bringing a new franchisee into the system should be approached with care. Applicants shouldn't be awarded a franchise just because they can write a check for the franchise fee. After all, they may not be right for the particular system. As a franchisor, would you want to have to lock your office doors, call the cops, and get a restraining order because a franchisee with no experience bought six franchises at once and is now pounding on your door like Dustin Hoffman in *The Graduate*? Instead of yelling the name of the girl he loves, he's yelling, "I'm going out of business! You suck!" Yes, this kind of thing has actually happened. The franchisor needs to make sure all parties involved in the franchise agreement know what they're getting into. When the franchise was sold to a new publicly traded entity, brought in some seasoned pros and got serious about interviewing prospective franchisees, the attitude and performance of current franchisees showed dramatic improvement within three years. Sales, margins and attitudes improved and why? We were all making money!

Of course, it goes both ways. As a prospective franchisee you should work in an operation first and also interview current franchisees. Try to call on some who have been in the system a short time as well as experienced, battle-hardened ones. Would you like to have your mind boggled? Here are some true examples of franchisee fails. We had a father and son purchase a store, and they wanted to sell only baseball and softball equipment. That would be like McDonald's selling only burgers. No fries, no Cokes. We had another person buy a store who never said much of anything to customers unless they asked for help. He had no music in the store, either. "Hello, would you like to shop in a graveyard?" We had multiple franchisees buy a store for a family member—usually an unqualified family member. The franchisee would never visit their own store. We had many franchisees that didn't attend the twice-yearly national conferences or regional meetings. "I've had plenty of schooling, so I don't need to ever go back and learn anything ever again." And every one of these franchisees complained loudly and sent out all kinds of bad, misleading communication to the franchisor and to fellow franchisees about why their business was doing poorly and why the franchisor was at fault. When asked whether they were spending the right amount on advertising or were using the new computer reports or were planning to go to conferences or workshops to improve their hiring and best practices, the answer was almost always, "No, that stuff doesn't work for me."

So let's get this straight—you bought a franchise, which means you bought their concept and unique way of doing business, but you refuse to even try or attempt a fifty to seventy-five percent participation rate in all the resources provided to you by said franchise and your business is failing? You thoroughly researched the franchise, abandoned your career, invested your life savings, risked your current and future family's financial future, and you will not participate in or try the new resources provided to you by said franchisor?

Popular wisdom says, "Stupid is as stupid does." So, to wrap up, evaluate yourself, the concept, and the franchisor. Make sure it's all a good match. Ask for everything you can from your franchisor but remember they are not there to guarantee your success.

Now there are lots of "bad boys" in every business group. Franchisors are not perfect. Ours was far from it. But a sincere effort on the part of franchisees and franchisors to keep improving is the environment for a successful business model—and a valuable asset when it's time for you to sell. Cha-ching!

Highlights

1.   Franchises are great at helping you build business acumen.
2.   All franchises are not the same. Do your research.
3.   Make sure they are growing and providing a way for you to grow.
4.   When you commit, you must be "all-in" committed to their system.

3

How to Get Started When Money Is Scarce

Turning dead ends into cul-de-sacs

HOW DOES ONE build something with nothing? In my case, how did I start a business with almost no money? I took stock of my assets and made a plan and started working my plan. Just like the Bible story of the fishes and the loaves feeding the multitudes, assets to start and grow your business will many times appear from seemingly nowhere. Assets that were there but you never realized you had them. In the following you'll read how I—and others—found our hidden assets. Many times, that hidden asset was attitude!

When I first had my "Thunderbolt" idea, I took my plan to my extended family—the family who might have money to invest, anyway. After being denied there, then presenting my plan to any friends who might be able to invest, I had no takers. Most of my peers were like me—just getting started in life, and every penny earned was spent on living, which meant partying and rent. I remember being frustrated, then resigned that my plan would never happen.

I knew from early on I wanted to build a business. I was twenty-five when my dad died, and I thought I would inherit the forty acres on which he was living. Little did I know he was paying for the land like a sharecropper. There was no loan with a bank. He had signed an agreement with the landowner that was little more than rent to own. Dead end. I was frustrated by this debacle and lack of help from family members. But sometimes answers are right in front of you, literally, and I did get help from a family member. It came in the form of a sticky note—a simple sticky note on a bathroom mirror in my cousin's home. While visiting him, I saw this yellow Post-it note on the mirror that read: "If it is to be…it's up to me." The Lord works in mysterious ways. In the end, I realized my family did help me. Because I didn't get any support, I got really pissed off. Not at them so much as the world trying to hold me back. I needed that rejection to reach down deep and find my true grit. "If it is to be…it's up to me" is true. I thought I was at a dead end. I didn't realize I was actually in a cul-de-sac.

Two weeks later I got a call from a former colleague who had hired me for my first job out of college. We'd stayed in touch, and I'd presented my plan to him earlier. He had been mulling it over. Maybe he saw the energy, passion, and positive attitude I had. Maybe he liked the recycling aspect of the franchise concept. He and I were always anti-establishment, independent types. We began talking about the actual nuts and bolts of how we would build this business. I had $20,000 from my dad's estate. He had his parents' investments we could borrow against, plus $10,000 of his own money. After more questions we put together THE PLAN. I came whipping out of that cul-de-sac like a NASCAR driver on a banked track!

Our business plan had our target customers, target geography for store, travel patterns, projected region growth, estimated sales, marketing, starting inventory, first year expenses (no salary), loan repayment projection, and we projected everything for five years.

It looked good. Really good. Even our bios and resumes and philosophy on this particular business at this particular time in history looked good. We used this as our template to get our loan. And it worked! Gulp. *Oh crap, what do we do now?* With this loan approval, we now had permission to jump off a cliff! We now had a chance to go into debt up to Jack and the Beanstalk's eyeballs with nothing but some ink on a piece of paper. YES! Then the adrenaline of having a mission kicked in. As the Blues Brothers said, "A mission from God!"

So that begs the question—how does one accomplish a mission from God? And by the way, if you don't feel, I mean REALLY feel, you are on a mission of some sort, you have absolutely no business going into business. This relates directly to your greatest asset. Attitude. It would be like if we "kinda sorta" wanted to go to the moon one day. You'll never get there. See scene of rocket blowing up on the launch pad.

But a true mission starts with a list. Was the universe built with a list? I don't know, but that's the way it works on earth. Just start making the list. Then you can prioritize and delegate. My partner, Glen, and I were great at making lists. When I met Glen, his office had lists for his lists. Sticky notes everywhere. We divided our lists under four major subjects: operations, inventory, marketing, and staff. I took responsibility for operations and marketing, and he was responsible for inventory and staff hiring. Plus, we were buying a franchise so they even provided us with more lists. Whee! But for every item on a to-do list there is a sub-list. Double whee! We were on our way to operating our very own business!

But wait! What if you didn't have a friend appear who was willing and able to fund you or partner with you? Another dead end? No, let's look at other ways to turn this dead end into a cul-de-sac moment.

Today, there are a crazy amount of different ways to access funding, probably more than at any time in the history of humans. There are traditional banks, SBA loans, private lenders, home equity loans, credit cards, crowdfunding, micro funding, angel investors, purchase order financing, and vendor financing. I am probably missing some. Most businesses today have used many of these sources, sometimes all at the same time. And here's the golden rule of asking for money—be prepared. I'm an outdoorsy person, and one of my favorite sayings is, "There is no such thing as bad weather, only poorly prepared participants." The same goes for applying for funding. This is the minimum of what you need:

1. Three years of personal tax returns.
2. References, personal and professional.
3. A complete business plan. That means five-year profit and loss (P&L) projections, market study, competition study, marketing plan, detailed breakdown of how the funding is to be spent, and time line of how the money will be repaid with an assumed interest rate. For help with a business plan (I'd never created one before), go to SCORE.org (the Service Corps of Retired Executives) and it's FREE. https://atlanta.score.org/resource/business-plan-template-startup-business.
4. Personal statement, reason for starting this business, bio, and resume.
5. Be ready to sign a personal guarantee. Your spouse may also need to sign.
6. Perhaps establish a letter of credit and/or use your personal home as collateral.

Later in business, as you need additional funding to grow, not much of this will change except lenders and investors will also want to see business tax returns. As you establish your business, the requirements for personal guarantees will fall away.

These dead ends that become cul-de-sac moments occur during every business's life span, no matter how big or how small your business, and they all need cash to execute their turnaround.

An example of a mature large company executing an excellent cul-de-sac moment would be when the Coca-Cola Company introduced New Coke. They quickly realized they'd made a dead-end decision and used the return to the old recipe to create momentum, resulting in a huge PR win and increased sales. Making a dead-end decision is not the recommended way to increase sales but serves as a great example of a great comeback. Other well-known examples are turnarounds by Apple, Starbucks, GM, Delta, and Airbnb. Whether it was Steve Jobs returning to a struggling Apple after being kicked out of his own company ten years earlier or Richard Anderson taking over Delta Airlines after it emerged from bankruptcy (not to mention merging it with Northwest Airlines and also buying an oil refinery), what I've found consistent in these stories is the return of a leader or current leadership that has to take the company to what I call a "Scarlet O'Hara" moment. Talk about an attitude moment. In this *Gone with the Wind* scene that occurs at the end of the first half of the movie before intermission, Scarlett is silhouetted against a hot, burning Georgia sunset. Starving, she digs in the hard, red clay and finds herself gnawing the last dirty potato to survive. She looks to the sky and declares, "As God is my witness, I will NEVER go hungry again!"

There are those times when you just have to "will" things to happen. Everything around you seems to be going nowhere. There is no energy. There's a real sense of resignation. To turn this dead-end situation into a cul-de-sac, you must look at those bankers, board members, and employees and say, "Get off your ass and let's do this!"

When looking for my first position in Atlanta, I interviewed at CNN. Many of their offices, including security, were literally in trailers. Small signs with messages of motivation and encouragement had been cut and taped to the walls. It was as if founder Ted Turner had personally come in and posted them. The one I'll never forget said, "If you can't find anything to do, GO HOME." Ted's success story of cash flow battles is historic. He definitely turned many a dead-end moment into a cul-de-sac.

Every company has these moments. Like any speed bump in life, it's not "if" but "when" and how you handle them that creates the magic—your demeanor, presence, and attitude. How do you respond to board members? How do you respond to employees? How do you respond to customers? Prepare for this so when a dead-end moment comes along you won't be surprised. It will be a "knowing" moment in your career, and you'll have the attitude to find the hidden assets.

Highlights

1. Get creative and look for "assets" you didn't know you had.
2. Start asking questions and listen. People really do love to share.
3. Create a well-thought-out business plan and follow that plan.
4. As Winston Churchill said, "Never, never, never, give up."

4

Marketing Starts with Your People

But first, "pre-market" your brain

PRE-MARKETING? IS THAT the time spent sharpening your pencils? Researching which sign you're going to hang out in front of your business? Choosing the colors for your logo, letterhead, and team shirts? Well, the following chapter offers thoughts on traditional marketing along with what you, the Chief Market Positioner, must recognize within yourself.

Pre-marketing is what you must do inside your head when you are elevated to, or about to elevate yourself to, the status of "Grand Poobah," "Big Cheese," CEO, CFO, or CIO. When you own or operate a business, everything you do, wear, respond, emote, shrug, wink, and slouch at reflects the attitude of the endeavor. And you know what? It sucks. Some days you just want to throw on a T-shirt, flip-flops, and play Jimmy Buffett.

Yes, in certain industries you can do your best Zuckerberg and wear a hoodie all the time. But even he understands the nature of consistency and the power of example to your vendors, employees, and investors. There always comes a day when you have to put on a suit and appear before Congress.

So how does this attitude transformation occur inside your newly self-crowned "Grand Poobah" mind? I don't have a specific answer. Some just get it. They've been mentored directly or indirectly through previous bosses or family. Some still don't get it even after being surrounded by the best. You'll witness certain indicators that a person is uncomfortable with leadership. They don't get to their own meetings on time. They take on tasks or assign tasks but never set a timetable and don't follow up on progress. They're always too busy for the actual people who will execute the details of the business. Like a rosebush in trouble, you start seeing brown spots, leaves fall off, and there's some kind of spiderweb attached under the leaves.

The specific answer I do know is this: If the attitude in your head is not right, if you have not fully "pre-marketed" your brain to embrace being the leader *all the time*, it will be reflected in the attitude of everyone.

Think of your own situations. Have you been in a work environment where you felt good energy overall? Were employees getting along? Tasks managed on time? Employees jumping in to help with difficult vendors or clients? Or did they stall by trying to ask questions they could probably figure out and answer on their own? Was there a general sense of pride in working for this business? You know what it feels like when things aren't going well, so don't fool yourself when it comes to running your own business. Your customers and vendors will know it. I noticed at one point my employees were taking off their work shirt before heading out to lunch. They were not proud of where they worked. It hurt. But I made a point to ask them at the next company meeting how we could foster pride in our business. What businesses did they know of where people were proud to work? What could we do to develop more pride? Pride in where you work is wonderful marketing. As the leader, make sure you "pre-market" your head. Once you've got your head right, then we can truly talk marketing!

What's the best marketing tool? Word of mouth. Every business owner and advertising guru will tell you that. Now, we have the largest word-of-mouth technology in the history of the planet with Facebook, Google, Yelp, Instagram, etc. Plus, we have amazing ways to collect and analyze the data feedback provided from all these marketing platforms. So the best way to get good word-of-mouth advertising is to provide a good experience. Today, that experience has to extend into all our media platforms too. And whose responsibility is that? Yours, sometimes, but your staff's most of the time. That's why the pre-marketing part of this chapter is so important. If your attitude does not resonate with and transfer to your employees, then you and your company might get a negative or inconsistent reputation. As every retailer, restaurant, and service out there tries to create the best "experience" for their customers, I advise you to embrace marketing ideas and push them as far as possible. Don't hold back. Ever! People want to watch other people do crazy things they would never do in public. Creative marketing creates a buzz and an atmosphere that this is where things are happening—that this business, whether it's a law firm or a kid's party facility, is at the top of its industry. George Lois, the advertising guru who wrote the book *Damn Good Advice (for people with talent!)*, was asked to define advertising. He replied, "Advertising is poison gas. It should bring tears to your eyes, unhinge your nervous system, and knock you out!"[1] I love that.

In a wonderful collaborative effort, franchisees, the Play It Again Sports franchisor, and the franchise advisory council (franchisees elected by their peers), created the concept of "Everybody Plays!" If Nike can say "Just Do It," then we are "The Official Sponsor of Everyone Who Plays." It's a sports store. Yes, pull it out! Try it on! Let's try it out right now. Young, old, everyone—let's have fun and play! A few stores were already doing this type of interactive experience with their customers, resulting in increased sales, better margins, and better word of mouth as evidenced by their social media statistics. The stores with incentives for their employees to be engaging and interactive saw their "likes" go up. The average time on their websites increased and overall engagement with the community rose. We suggested owners install bells to ring or horns to toot. Cool shoes? Ring the bell! It's your birthday? Ring the big orange bell! This is your first ball glove? Ring the bell, baby! I incentivized employees by creating contests encouraging them to seek out customers to interact with. Maybe even get a video with the customer "playing" to post on our social media channels. Any reason whatsoever to create some fun and make people feel special because they are! We "leaders" get so caught up in our goals and things to do, we forget to see the unique opportunities within our own businesses.

So, here's one contest that falls under the theme of "best idea never executed." As we were a new *and* used sporting goods store, most every equipment bag brought in by a kid's mom had a—yes, come on, guess—a used jockstrap in the bottom. I'm talking the good old-fashioned strappy jocks with the wide waistband and thin little straps up around the back. Lots of stains, etc. You get the picture. A slingshot. Sorry for the picture I just put in your head. And naturally the mom would be embarrassed. "Oh, dear! I didn't clean out the bag! How did that get in there?" So, of course you've got to have fun with this. Why throw it away when you can do marketing? We planned to gather the largest collection of used jockstraps, contain them in plexiglass, and notify Guinness World Records. For the reveal we would have had a PR extravaganza and invited CNN, ESPN, local radio, TV, etc. (There was no social media then.) The jockstrap-counting official would have worn a hazmat suit. Of course there would have been a contest to guess the number of jockstraps we'd collected. The winner would have received a free trip somewhere. We'd keep the display for a time, then blow up the container on live TV, preferably in the middle of a football field on homecoming night. You can see it, right? Jockstraps flying through the air, landing softly on the homecoming court's tiaras.

In ad agency lingo, it had legs! It was a marketing campaign that could literally be rolled out for multiple memorable events—think Chick-fil-A cows and "Dilly Dilly" Bud Light. But it never happened. Why? I didn't prioritize it. Like a lot of small business owners, day after day, the little things that steal time pulled me away. After I got my business started, I fell into the same excuse trap that keeps many of us from starting a new business venture in the first place. So make marketing a priority!

What I did execute well was a consistent advertising plan. Many franchisors will require you to spend a percentage of gross sales on your local store marketing. But even if there is no requirement, you should set one for yourself—internet ads, direct mail, radio, TV, cable, even hiring a marketing agency. Whatever you decide to implement, be consistent. Running any campaign one time will not show results. Be consistent for at least two years. This gives you a year of results and a second year of comparable results. These results include sales performance and your data-gathering social media and website performance. These measurables let you know if you are on the right track. Depending on what you're selling, your potential clients may not need what you sell for quite a while in the future, but you have been consistently in their minds. When they need your product or service, they think of you. Then use your data to tweak your budgets, tweak your message, tweak your marketing platforms and data collection. Now you're marketing!

As a start-up we were very cautious about our budgets. Based on my ad agency and owner experience, I highly recommend spending your budget in a way that makes an impact. For me that meant saving up three months of my advertising budget and spending it all in ten days. I would run a combo of local cable, local print, and some special internet ads on top of my regular internet presence, then wait ninety days. I'd save up three more months of my budget and do it again. People would come in two months after the campaign and say, "I just saw your ad!" The ad campaign made a memorable impression, and when they were ready to shop, they thought of me. The takeaway is, be memorable and be consistent. The other advertising downfall business owners get into is looking for quick, measurable results from their ad spend. Sometimes you get an immediate bump in sales, but many times you won't. Don't abandon your plan. Stick with it for two years to get real measurables. The number one measurable result is you're still in business! Imagine if Coca-Cola stopped spending on advertising for six months. What a windfall profit to their bottom line! No one would ever say they could forget Coca-Cola, but Coca-Cola knows those who stop marketing start sliding backward. Even if you're an accountant or undertaker, there is low-cost marketing you can implement.

I have a son in the film industry in Los Angeles. One day we were discussing why a movie did so well in testing before audiences, had the best marketing and distribution ever for the company, and yet bombed at the box office. One of the key questions asked of audiences at a test showing is,

"Would you recommend this to your friends?" It's classic word-of-mouth advertising, and more than eighty-five percent of those who saw the movie said "yes." This particular movie was about dogs. A majority of people in this country own dogs. The movie was well produced, fun, and had a happy ending, a perfect Hollywood format. What the producers forgot was research showings are free and most attendees were dog owners and it was a nice sweet movie. Yes, we'll recommend it to our friends. The reality was, when the audience walked out of the theater, they had a nice, gentle, glow. *Nice.* Not "Wow, did you see that scene?" They didn't leave remembering, "I was scared or crying or heart-thumping excited" at some point in the movie. People will talk about something that takes them a little "over the top." It can be as simple as Chick-fil-A employees saying, "It's my pleasure" to their customers, rather than "Thank you." You go in now for that yummy chicken sandwich and lemonade and can't wait to hear them say, "It's my pleasure." Movie scripts need something a bit over the top to get people talking. Did the character or characters do something you have always wanted to do in a situation? Did you punch the bully in the nose? Did you throw mama from the train? Did you hold the girl's hand when everyone was looking? In this tough market where everyone has Facebook, Instagram, and LinkedIn feeds full of video ads, does your product or service have a little "over the top" to it?

My vision statement that influenced my decisions, especially marketing, was "The Neatest Coolest Whizzbang Sports Store on the Planet!" When pondering a decision, whether it pertained to new inventory, employee training, marketing, or whatever, many times I would think, "What is going to push us closer to being The Neatest Coolest Whizzbang Sports Store on the Planet?

Here are some great examples of business leaders who never forgot to create distinct visions in their company: Ted Turner, Richard Branson, and Henry Ford. At the inauguration of CNN, Turner said this about the new network: "...its international coverage and greater depth coverage will bring both in the country and in the world a better understanding of how people of different nations work together."[2] Branson's vision in business is: "Know how to be a good leader and always try to bring out the best in people."[2] Ford had a global vision with utilitarian consumerism as the key to peace. [3] I'm sure there are lots of CEO stories that never make the light of day, stories where the leader took everyone by surprise by saying, doing, or wearing something that shook up the room. Something that strategically communicated to everyone: "Don't get too comfortable. I'm looking for innovation."

Now I'm not suggesting if you own a funeral home you rig the body to sit up and wave and say, "Goodbye, I love you, thanks for the flowers!" That might be funny in a Will Ferrell movie, but you know your business and, even more important, you should know your competitor's business. You have to outperform them, "perform" being the key word. Your business platform is a stage. Engage your noodle and ask questions to everyone around you, even your kids if you have kids. What can you do that's "over the top"? This attitude recognition within yourself will establish the "pre-marketing" your brain needs and will give your employees direction as they carry out your actual day-to-day "marketing." And they will never want to take off their company shirt again!

Highlights

1. You're the boss. Make sure your attitude is right. All the time.
2. Keep your marketing efforts consistent. And don't stop. Even when you're at the top.
3. Think in interactive ways. Engage customers, employees, and vendors.
4. Take good ideas and push them in crazy, over-the-top ways. Don't make more good vanilla ice cream!

5

First Year Profit, Cash Flow

And X-wing fighters[1]

NO LIE—MY business partner and I were so naïve about profit and loss statements we thought the money listed on the bottom line of our business plan's profit and loss statement would actually be money in the bank at the end of the year. Ha ha! Coming up are a few anecdotes about how great sales don't always mean a great cash situation and tips on preparing yourself ahead of time for the inevitable cash flow crunch.

Our background was basically project management. Here is your project. Here is your budget. Execute and after all invoices are paid and monies are collected you would have money left over at the end of the project. Well a business certainly runs the same, right? Each year is basically a project to be managed. Well, sort of. We didn't realize profit would get sucked off the bottom line in real cash flow terms with silly things like debt or reinvesting in inventory.

"Hey, look! We've got lots more assets! We've got lots of profit! We've got lots more inventory! We've got retained earnings! We're doing great! Oh, sh*t! We're poor! And we owe a truckload of taxes!" Now we really came to know what it feels like to be a farmer. You feel like you're getting screwed! Land rich and cash poor, as a farmer would say.

To be clear, the P&L is a financial statement that summarizes your revenues and expenses for a certain period, and it's important. But the cash flow statement is what really helps you manage your stress level on a week-to-week basis. The cash flow statement reports the sources and uses of cash for a certain period and is used in conjunction with the P&L. It can help you project future cash needs based on current conditions, and that projection is critical to your planning. This is also critical to managing your stress level because high stress is directly proportional to the amount of unknown and unplanned events in your business.

This was the reality check at the end of our first year. Yes, it could have been worse. We could have had no profit, lower assets, less inventory, and money in the bank to pay less in taxes. And we would've been going out of business.

But it is one hell of a buzzkill to realize you've worked your butt off and you're effectively broke. Your accountant's advice will sound something like this: "Well, you've just got to work a little harder now to pay those taxes." We were so naïve. We did not have a business or accounting background. We could've used a mentor. We were a franchisee, so we figured the franchisor would be our mentor. (Beware, fellow franchisees. See "**Questions to Ask or Research about a Potential Franchisor**" in the appendix.) The question to ask your franchisor and your accountant is, "Do you provide financial analysis training?" If they don't and you still really love the franchise concept, get some training on your own. Online and community colleges are great. Just understand what you don't know.

I've learned that when it comes to dealing with cash flow, relationship-building, strategic precision, and discipline are the magic steps that lead to profit. For example, if you have big preseason orders of inventory arrive and the bills aren't due for several months, immediately schedule a weekly partial pay down on those invoices. Better yet, escrow a portion in an interest-bearing money market account toward these invoices every week. Also, to ensure you have cash available, establish a line of credit with a bank. If your vendors allow them, you can even use business credit cards where you can earn points but be sure to pay the credit cards off in full. Having several forms of cash flow relief are essential, but thousands of business owners don't do it. It's ok to stray outside your cash flow plan during your monthly or quarterly operating decisions; however, do it strategically with a plan to roll the unexpected spending into your overall cash flow statement.

For example, let's say you didn't plan to invest in new inventory SKUs for the season, but you have a vendor introducing a product that a few customers have heard about and asked if you're going to start carrying it. You go for it and place an order. That invoice will come due in thirty days and so will your preseason inventory invoice. Your profits from the preseason inventory are paying for the new product. So, when it comes time to pay the rent and payroll, you've already spent your profit on new inventory that's sitting on the shelf, and you're short on cash. Your cash to pay your operating bills got reassigned to that shelf, and cash flow has slowed down. Ah, cash flow—my favorite term. Flow, flow, flow your business gently down the stream. No flow, no go. If you plot this cash going down versus sales going up on a chart, it makes an "X."

That brings us to the magic of short-term debt, and the meditative relief of understanding the wisdom of short-term debt versus long-term debt. Taking on either short-term debt (such as credit cards or vendor financing) or long-term debt (think of loans over three years), is not good or bad. They are just different financing tools used for different jobs. Screwdriver or hammer, get the right tool for the job. I would consult your CPA. Take a long-term look at your short-term potential cash needs because you *will* need cash at some point. The stereotypical rule in banking is when you don't need money, bankers are easy lenders. When times get tough, they don't want to lend, and they make loan terms more difficult. It's essential to establish a relationship with lenders before you need their money. Hence, the old adage: Banks will loan you an umbrella on a sunny day but want it back when it begins to rain. Plan ahead.

As a result, in year two, my business partner and I started planning ahead. We secured a line of credit from the bank, which we drew from when we had cash flow slowdowns during normal business cycles. We paid off the line of credit during good cash flow times. When you walk into a bank armed with your recent tax return, P&L statement, cash flow statement, and a well-thought-out written plan describing how you will use the credit, the banker will love you! As a relatively new business owner, they will want to attach some or all of your business assets to the line of credit and even some personal ones as well. Ask the banker what's required to reduce or eliminate the attached asset requirements.

So how does the flight pattern of the X-wing fighter in *Star Wars*[2] pertain to cash flow? Glad you asked! This is just a fun way to think about it. Have you ever noticed how the X-wing fighter prepares for different types of flight? Pull up a quick YouTube video if you need a refresher. When the X-wing fighter needs to travel smooth and fast, it folds its wings flat. This is prime position for intergalactic hyperdrive warp speed. When the X-wing fighter starts to engage in close combat, it unfolds its wings to form the X. It slows immediately and is forced to be more maneuverable if it wants to survive. Your business's cash flow versus sales growth works the same way.

Basic cash flow–when sales go up, cash on hand goes up, and inventory goes down. When put together on a time graph, they form an X. When sales go up, the immediate impulse is to buy more inventory because you want more sales. So you use your profit to buy *even more* inventory than you did the first time. However, if not monitored carefully, the X gets inverted, which means inventory and sales go up and cash goes down. Here's why: If you have huge increases in sales, you are constantly using up your cash to buy more inventory to keep sales going up. Soon, you'll run out of cash to pay invoices on time, and sales will be forced to eventually slow down. Unless, of course, you borrow. If you don't want to borrow or can't and you want to grow organically, those huge increases in sales will eventually force your sales to slow down. In this situation you've had to slow down and open up the wings on your X-wing fighter and get maneuverable. I found this to be true, and we'll talk even more about it in the next chapter. Also, a good accountant should provide you with a cash flow statement and advice on growth plans based on your cash positions. The website AccountingCoach.com explains cash flow analysis and how cash flow relates to growth strategies and other financial statements very well. Also, ask your franchisor if they provide cash flow training. (See the appendix of the book on questions to gain wisdom.)

I discovered if my sales grew over ten percent one year, the next year I had a flat sales year of maybe one or two percent sales growth. It's kind of like the business was drawing a big gasp of air to keep growing. All businesses are a bit different, but in my retail environment this was the case. After the third or fourth year I understood the process, and my anxiety dramatically decreased. Knowledge also gave me control. Mental control. We small business people love control. So, understand how your X-wing fighter plane of a business maneuvers. Keeping your wings in a flatter X-pattern is better for consistent straightforward flight because you won't be forced to maneuver quite so drastically to keep from crashing. You will go on to destroy the Death Star and save the princess!

Highlights

1. Lots of sales don't always mean lots of cash.
2. Secure alternate operating cash sources before you need them.
3. Create disciplined accounts payable procedures.
4. Understand the sales cycles of your industry. Plan cash needs accordingly.
5. Get a certified public accountant (CPA), not just a bookkeeper, who provides all the right tools: P&L, balance sheet, cash flow statement, auditing, and strategic advice.
6. Take a course on cash flow and expense management.

6

Cash Flow as You Grow

"Whee, it's a roller coaster!"

THIS IS WHERE the real fun in business happens. Your feet are wet. If you've made it to year two or three, you just might have a viable business. Year two's profit and loss compared to year one's is mildly interesting. Were your initial hunches correct? Were they a fluke? Year three you really get your teeth into some comparable numbers based on your specific business and industry cycles. Real, strategic plans and goals can be mapped out for years four and five. In this chapter, I'll share more growing pains because after year three we owners got a bit cocky. We tried to grow too fast. But everything is still dependent on my favorite waitress at Mel's Diner. Flo. Yes, flow, as in cash flow.

In the previous chapter I focused on cash flow to inventory. Now I'll speak to cash flow needs for maturing operations. I built my teeny-tiny business without any outside financing other than our initial start-up capital. Ours was a retail store that depended on having inventory on hand to grow our business, so cash flow was critical on a week-to-week basis. I knew nothing of the intricacies or theories of cash flow or its effects on other parts of my balance sheet. All I knew was we needed to have enough on hand to meet payroll, bills due that week, and tax withholding deadlines. After all, what else does a chief financial officer really have to worry about?

Well, it turns out they worry about a lot. CFOs are responsible for cash flow, tax liabilities, reporting to shareholders, accounts payable, accounts receivable, and according to the Deloitte CFO Signals survey as reported in the *Wall Street Journal* October 2017, CFOs are most worried about "technology disruption and talent challenges."[1] So, you've got that going for you! As the owner, you need to keep in mind all the other hats you wear—how do we make cash flow less of a beast?

I was an adult leader in the Boy Scouts for fifteen years. I taught leadership and led at the unit, district, and council levels. We taught leadership courses for youth and adults that gave participants the skills needed to lead an all-volunteer organization. The best of these courses is called Wood Badge for the 21st Century. Despite its name, the course was all about leadership, and whether we were on a trail and someone got hurt or there was a personality conflict between committee members, we had a motto: "Use your assets." I mentioned this in the introduction, but I'm repeating the lesson here because we always forget stuff. "Use your assets" means stop, take a look around, and evaluate your group and situation. You have the means to beat this challenge, if you just get creative and pay attention to what you're about to do. Managing the cash needs of your business is no exception.

For example, when I found myself in the middle of a cash-crunch crisis, I took short-term cash advances on my personal credit cards several times to make payroll. It's tough and embarrassing to admit I had to resort to such desperate measures. The good news is there are a lot more financing avenues available for small businesses now. A quick internet search will bring up a slew of options; however, I like to stay local, if possible, and this is where your networking groups really pay off.

If you anticipate falling behind on invoices, staying in touch with the vendors where you have accounts payable owed is huge! This is especially important with government entities like the IRS and the state department of revenue, not to mention your landlord. Just a phone call or email once a week lets them know you are on top of the issues. You will sleep better and won't dread the phone calls interrupting your day. When you think about it, the person responsible for collecting payments sits down at their desk every day with a "to-do" list staring at them. One of those is to call people who owe money. What a pain! But if you call them first or pick up the phone with a smile in your voice, what an amazing difference you're making in the relationship! If you can't pay the full balance this week or month, having a good relationship with the accounting departments of your vendors is especially invaluable. They will know you are solid and dependable, taking care of your business even if you do have a short-term cash crunch. Plus, when you're ready to grow, they will be more likely to extend more credit and better terms because they know how you operate when times are tough. My financial obligations were always met, and my business continued to grow. These are the signs of a successful businessperson. Like a true marathoner, you've got to embrace the "suck."

Ever notice how if you cut down a tree and study its rings they're not a consistent width? The tighter the rings, the sturdier and harder the wood. More width between the rings indicates a good year for water and fast growth. I noticed something similar in my business around year eight. When my business grew at a twenty percent increase one year, the following year our sales were flat. The next year we would again grow ten to twenty percent, followed by a slightly flat year. This was due to the business growing organically. We relied on the profit generated to grow. The seed money was plowed back into the farmland of inventory, but then we had to pay the bills. Growing a business is the equivalent of stopping to catch your breath, get a drink of water, or suck down an orange during a marathon. Good marathoners know you can grab small amounts of these while you run, and you don't have to stop. There is a time and a place for infusions of outside cash. But as small business owners we are so afraid to take on more debt. What was I afraid of? I didn't even know what and what not to be afraid of.

I do know that the inside of a business is not the outside. I have an extremely successful friend who told me a story about his business. He was interviewing a prospect to head up a new sales division. The potential employee asked him about a picture in his office. It was a framed cover of a national business magazine, touting my friend's company as one of the top 100 up-and-coming businesses. The cover was from twelve years earlier, and the business was actually a different business at the time of the article. The prospect was so impressed, and it helped excite him about coming to work for this firm. My friend revealed to me that at the time the article came out and they were taking the photo for the cover, he knew the company was doomed and would be reorganizing in less than four months. Of course, they must they have been doing something right to get the attention of the national business media, but the article became the office joke. The company did reorganize and has since become very successful. But the message is clear: Take care of your core or you will rot from the inside out.

After five years in business I'm feeling cocky. Now I really know what I'm doing, right? I have two locations, and it's time to ramp up to my long-term goal of getting eight to ten locations, then selling them. I have a good track record, and the banks are begging to lend. In the next eighteen months, I opened two new locations and relocated one of the others. This is when I really needed a mentor, although I didn't know I needed one. I thought I knew what I was doing! I was on the ride of my life!

Little did I know the ride was a roller coaster, and I was about to take that big drop—the one where your stomach floats up into your throat and you're not sure what's happening then you hit the bottom and your face gets all pinched up and you're gritting your teeth and you just hope the testing engineers were there that week tightening all the bolts on this thing. Did you know if you have three locations, you have the same logistics, employee, operations, and advertising/marketing issues as if you had ten locations? That represents cash and people flow with a capital F. I learned this the hard way. I had grown two stores by investing about $250,000 in each to get them up and running. Once they were successfully operating for three or four years, I thought I would open two more the same way— borrow $250K for each store and follow the successful plan again. The problem arises when you realize the unaccounted-for effect on business operations when you, the owner, go from being in a location fifty percent of the time, then reduce it to twenty-five percent or less. So many nuanced issues don't get accomplished, implemented, or followed up on. Examples include employee training, maintenance, cleaning, overall employee attitude, employee honesty, and communication with you and your team. I took eight years to build a great business and crashed it in two. Then I took another ten to dig myself out and rebuild. What would I have done differently? I would have borrowed more money as part of my expansion costs to hire older and more seasoned professional employees as managers. In the first two stores I hired young, great attitude go-getters and promoted from within, but their relationships with the employees became more like friendships than employees and managers. The young managers I hired could not hold all their fellow employees to high-enough standards.

KIND Snacks had a similar path where the business was growing like wild before having all systems in place for stable growth. As reported in *USA Today*, owner Daniel Lubetzky spent too much time trying to rapidly grow the company before he got his product right. Nearly bankrupt, he then spent two years improving the product. Afterward, he was able to attract $20 million in funding, which provided stability to grow effectively for the long-term. In 2014 he bought his company back.[2]

Crumbs Bake Shop had a different ending. The business started in 2003 and the *Wall Street Journal* described it as the biggest cupcake vendor in the world when it went public in 2011. *Inc.* magazine said it was also one of the fastest-growing with dozens of stores. It grew too fast and became burdened with debt from maintaining physical locations. Shifting consumer tastes created inconsistent demand. Crumbs Bake Shop struggled and closed the last stores in 2017.[3]

I'm sure these organizations had people with more official education and letters behind their name than I do. I know they made decisions based on the data on hand. But I ask myself, what questions did they not ask? What answers did they ignore? Asking a lot more questions might have saved me from driving bank to bank hoping to use my wife's credit card to get a cash advance to cover payroll. Asking questions might have saved me from lying awake in bed listening to a car drive down our street and wondering if it was the department of revenue coming to take our home. What if I had asked, "What does a rollout of five more stores over an eight-year span need in the way of cash, people, and time?" What if I had asked follow-up questions: "How and who will finance this? Have I had a conversation with my current banker and accountant about plans like that? What kind of people will I need for an expanded organization? Where am I going to find such people?" These questions seem obvious now and would have saved me hundreds of thousands of dollars. If you're reading this, then I commend you on being smarter than I was. I needed someone to throw these cold-water questions in my face.

There are now great cheap and free online tutorials about cash flow, the budgeting process for smart growth, and how to integrate multiple financial tools. Check out Investopedia.com, Merchantmaverick.com, and the KahnAcademy.org. Bonus points to you when you speak to a loan officer or private equity group, and they see you have cash flow "wisdom" and understand cash is needed for operations growth as well as product and service growth. Understanding the cash flow roller-coaster cycle of your particular industry or concept will help you anticipate, and maybe not enjoy, the dips but remain at peace knowing you've planned to come zipping up the next climb! So, "Hey, Flow! How about some more coffee!"

Highlights

1. Don't get too cocky after a few years in business.
2. When a cash crisis looms, look around and evaluate all your assets.
3. When growing locations, understand it takes more cash than when you started the first.
4. Stay in open, regular communication with vendors when in a cash crunch.
5. As the business grows, staffing requires more cash and more experienced employees.

7

Mentors

Yes, you need one

MEN-TOR: NOUN, AN "experienced or trusted advisor." As a verb, to "advise or train." If you are lucky enough to have a person like this in your life, count your blessings! A sympathetic, experienced businessperson to open up to is priceless. But you might have also heard of coaches or coaching for business owners. Is there a difference? Absolutely! Coaching is generally structured, the coach may or may not have knowledge in the same field as the "student," sessions are scheduled for a specific duration, and the coaches are paid for their time. Mentoring is often more informal, advice is offered at no charge, the mentor usually has significant knowledge and experience in the "student's" field, and the mentor's guidance may continue for years. Think of coaches as helping execute goals while mentors share strategy. Out of all the pieces of my business where I was successful in filling my pot of gold, finding a mentor was my biggest scab and scar. Even though I ended up mentoring five employees to go out and purchase their own businesses, I did not have a long-term mentor. Wow and ouch!

I cannot stress enough the importance of surrounding yourself with the right people. This is truly the way to turn dead ends into cul-de-sacs. Ask questions and find the right people and just maybe you won't find yourself in a dead end to start with.

Mentors guide you and help with overall strategy. They may not be able to answer every question, but they can help you find the right people to answer those other questions. For example, one attorney can't handle all legal issues. Leases and real estate require a real estate agent that exclusively represents you, not the landlord. Do all CPAs manage the same issues and work with all businesses or do they specialize in an industry? Government issues need advice. There are hundreds more. It's just experience. Situational wisdom. It's why contracts are so long. People, who most of the time are trying to gain an edge, have been asking these questions or forgetting to ask them since the Magna Carta was signed! Don't let lack of knowledge hold you back! This is where mentors come into play.

I'm a pretty confident do-it-yourself type of person. So ego and pride can get in the way. I don't ask for help easily. But I would have fewer scars and more pots of gold today if I had known how to ask for advice. And here's some advice for you: Even though you are positively, absolutely, one hundred percent zeroed in on the right way to do things and will not be shaken from your decisions, STOP!! Find a mentor and ask for guidance. Even if the questions seem dumb and you're certain you know the answers, finding a mentor (or several) for feedback on your ideas will give you even more confidence and validation when they confirm your path. Or they may keep you from making a big mistake. I never had this. I screwed up a lot. I guess I have a good attitude about making mistakes, and I'm successful because I managed to keep learning from them.

I should have found people who had larger businesses than mine and had grown them from the ground up. I should have asked them about cash flow needs. I should have asked them about people flow needs. I should have asked myself: What were my real goals? Did I want to make money or have a particular lifestyle? How long did I really want to commit to this enterprise? Smart people will connect you to other smart people. Every person I speak with now, no matter what their position is in life, I ask their advice. People love being needed, and I've learned an amazing amount. Please seek out experienced people and ask their advice. And just maybe you'll connect with a person who really wants to take you under their wing.

Now here's a guy that did it right. A young businessman I know was a collegiate golfer. He started a company that provides electronic signage boards for charity golf tournaments. He soon recognized the need for other services he could package for nonprofits, which are perpetually understaffed, short on volunteers, and low on budget. His business has grown well, but none of that impresses me as much as the informal group of business mentors he found and reached out to over and over again. I know his business has grown because of the group, not to mention his confidence going forward. Outstanding! He found great assets from experienced business people with situational wisdom.

There's a man I met by chance when I decided to start chartering sailboats for vacations. I needed a bit more training to get the proper certification to captain a 50-foot sailboat and be responsible for a couple of families' lives. I wanted chartering and coastal navigation training, so I chose a charter sailing school out of Tampa Bay. The other participants were a gentleman about seventy years old, his grown son, and the instructor. We proceeded to spend the next five days and nights together learning, sailing, taking practical and written tests, sleeping, cleaning, and eating in close quarters. I learned a lot about these people, especially the older man. He told me he'd hidden in a car trunk to escape communist East Germany right after the Berlin Wall was constructed. With only the clothes on his back, he came to America and is now one of the leading franchisees for a massive luxury hotel chain on the West Coast. He owns properties in Seattle and Hawaii. He has everything he wants and massive knowledge from a lifetime of learning. He has every reason to talk forever about everything he knows. But he doesn't. He asked questions constantly, not in a pestering way but curious and empathetic and genuine. He wanted to get to know me. He asked me questions *and he listened*. He knew more about me in just a few hours than I learned about him in three days. His desire to learn about people, who they are and what interests them, is sincere.

I believe this is a big reason he is so successful in business. He knows he can never have enough wisdom and knowledge about the human assets in his organization. So he shared his methods with me. For example, he gives the Briggs-Meyers personality questionnaire to everyone on his staff, whether they are cleaning people at his hotels or his top executives. I realized he is able to "mentor" all of his employees by helping them identify their strengths and weaknesses.

He confided that when taken properly and conducting a proper debriefing after the questionnaire, the results are quite enlightening. Many of these evaluations confirm what a lot of people already know about themselves. The structured conversations with the employee, before and after the evaluation, are how this business tool can launch an employee's motivation and effectiveness. It will give you, the owner, a full understanding of the human resource assets within your organization. Again, it's just another way this remarkable man takes the time and effort to get to know all of his employees. And employees are a business's greatest asset. Plus, they appreciate it! When was the last time you had a sit-down coffee with the person on your company's lowest rung? Upon getting back to my business after the sailing class, his counseling so motivated me that I made the test part of my training with employees. I even had my wife and kids take it too!

But my biggest takeaway from that sailing class was not learning coastal navigation. I learned how important it is to ask questions and *listen to the answers of people above and below me on the job ladder.* Despite that knowledge, I still find that hard to do when I meet people. This man made it look easy, but it isn't.

Some famous mentor-mentee relationships as described in *The Chronicle of Evidence Based Mentoring* include Oprah Winfrey, who was mentored by celebrated author and poet Maya Angelou, and Facebook CEO Mark Zuckerberg, who was mentored by former Apple CEO Steve Jobs. Actor-director Clint Eastwood credits his grandmother as his mentor, who told him "to always work hard and pursue his dreams."[1] I use these examples to show you even the most successful individuals seek mentoring and advice. No matter what level you are in an industry, there's probably a potential mentor in the room with you now, or someone who's benefiting from one. Go introduce yourself!

As you accumulate a massive to-do list to launch your business, remember to put finding a mentor on that list! How does one find mentors if, like me, you have no family or friends with this type of wisdom? Suck it up and ask for one! There are lots of small business mentor programs around now, and the internet is full of advice on where to find them. A great place to start is with your local business networking groups: the chamber of commerce, Rotary Club, SCORE (Service Corps of Retired Executives) is awesome; universities often have public-private business start-up incubator programs and even your state government has free programs. And don't forget to ask your banker! They want to see you succeed because you have to pay back that loan! Remember, people love to help someone with a positive ATTITUDE! Good people do business with good people they know.

This chapter began with the definition of mentor: a trusted advisor. But after you have worked with one for a while, I think you will revise that definition to "mentor: a way to gain confidence and a better night's sleep."

Highlights

1. Find a mentor!
2. Never stop asking questions.
3. You are never too smart or too successful to have a mentor.
4. Mentors help you with strategic thinking and direct you to additional resources.
5. Look for mentors through your local networking groups, chambers of commerce, SCORE, and other sources.

8

Making Decisions

The scariest thing in the woods!

FOLKS, I WOULD just like to warn you—I am that guy.

I am that guy who, after mowing the lawn, can be seen lying on the grass, staring up at who knows what—seeing shapes in the clouds or just noticing what shade of blue the sky is today. I am that guy who actually hugs trees. See, I'm outdoorsy. I love the woods and would rather sleep outside, in almost any kind of weather, than inside. As I mentioned earlier, one of my favorite sayings is, "There is no bad weather, only poorly prepared participants." Well, preparation starts with making decisions, and this next story will give you some keen insight into decision-making...paralysis.

How many of us like to hike or walk as recreation or hobby? I've heard walking is the number one recreational participant activity in the world.

Last year I hiked part of the Appalachian Trail for about three days. The trail is blessed with shelters every eight to ten miles or so. These shelters have been constructed off and on since the Great Depression, so the style and condition vary. Weekend hikers, like me, generally don't sleep in them; the shelters are for the "through hikers," the ones going all the way to Maine. The good thing about sleeping in shelters is you don't have to put up a tent, but you do have to sleep with stinky, snoring people who have all their own evening routines, etc. You get the picture—just set up the tent, brother.

But this time it was a beautiful evening, and there was no one around. So it seemed like a good opportunity to sleep in a shelter for the first time. I got my sleeping bag all set up with my cushy ground pad. I put my food up properly in the "bear bag" tree a good distance from camp. (The sites always attract critters because people always drop food. Food and other items we carry are "smellable" to critters. They create curiosity.) I'd also heard lots of stories about mice inhabiting the shelters for the same reasons. But how bad could it be, right? I'm a big boy. I'm a tough, woodsy dude who can handle a mouse running around. And the sun was going down fast.

So I'm all comfy in my sleeping bag on the wooden floor of the shelter, and it's dark. Dark. So dark I couldn't tell my eyes were open. I'm just starting to nod off when I hear a scratching waaay up in the rafters. No sweat, it's a mouse. Then I hear another. And another and my mind starts to wonder: *How many mice are up there? How big are they? Are they more like rats?* The scratching and scrabbling around seems, in my mind, to be coming from at least thirty mice, and they aren't slacking off. They're not like, "Shh, you might wake him up." I could just see them peeking over the rafters at me. One of them was tying on a bib. Another was holding silverware. Another was polishing his wine glass as they all got ready to scrabble on down and take a nibble off me. I lay there for about another two minutes then—bam! I grabbed my gear, and I was out of there! I set up my tent about fifty yards away and slept like a baby. When I woke up, I saw a mouse had gotten into my bear bag. A Houdini-type for sure.

"But Scott, where, oh where, is a business lesson in this?" you ask.

Well, think about it. There I was, lying in the dark, not taking any action, and trying to ignore the things that were bothering me. Of course, the more you ignore little things in your business, the more they grow, real or imagined, into nasty rats that can paralyze you with fear.

What are some issues that business owners ignore? Changing market conditions, certain technologies, cash flow needs, the IRS or state department of revenue, and human resources conflicts. Sometimes business owners ignore all of these at the same time, like those little mice peering over the rafters at you in the dark. Just waiting for a nibble.

For about eighteen months I had some issues withholding back taxes due to cash flow problems from trying to grow too fast. See how these things domino? Well everyone's afraid of the Big Bad Wolf—the IRS—right? But by taking quick action when I received IRS letters and actively engaging the agent assigned to me, we became good working partners. I set up a payment plan, and we worked through the issues. What's really interesting is halfway through the process, my first agent retired, and I got another agent from the personal individual tax side, who was new to business tax issues. Not only did I bring her up to speed on my case, I also taught her how to read a P&L and balance sheet. So many business owners get into worse trouble by ignoring billing issues. It's important to remember that people who work for the IRS sit at a desk every day with a job to do and a list of people to call. Just like you. It's the same thing with those nasty vendors calling to collect on invoices. If you can be the happy, easy-to-deal-with, and helpful call they have to make, you are golden.

Human resources issues (which is a nice way of saying employee drama) should never be ignored, but many times leaders take the attitude of, "Don't bother me. You're an adult—you figure it out!" I had a situation where an employee was telling other employees he was going to be the new manager soon. My conversation with him had been that I was evaluating staff to determine who the next manager would be, and he was a candidate. I also had another candidate, a longer-term employee who had come back after a two-month leave of absence. The friction between those two started to affect other staff. As soon as I got wind of the issue, I set them both straight with a face-to-face meeting to let each know exactly where they stood with me. It's like standing up in the dark and setting up a tent—I had to take action.

Sometimes taking action means doing fewer things inside or outside the business. Small business can be overwhelming; by backing off some commitments, you're able to breathe, focus, and regain control. Ash Ambirge's website, The Middle Finger Project, has some great tips for handling scary, overwhelming times. Here are a few: "1. Making and enforcing normal nine-to-five hours for a week or two. 2. Stop and analyze every project on your to-do list and see if the return on investment (ROI) is worth it. Can it be delegated? Or just dump it. 3. You're the boss, act like it (I could've used this one). You don't have to do everything. Just enforce your non-negotiables. 4. Get a change of scenery. When you're feeling there's just too much holding you down, these tips can help you get moving again." [1]

I was always slow to implement new technology or marketing plans. Yet every time we initiated these, I always wished we had started sooner. I would use cash flow or other reasons for holding back but being up front and engaging is part of learning. If you're not learning, you're not growing; if you're not growing, you're going out of business. Once again, taking action means there are fewer scary things in the woods you don't know about. That action could be making a few phone calls, having that uncomfortable face-to-face conversation, or running those budget numbers. As a society, we seem to be enthralled by the movies focused on "action": *Guardians of the Galaxy*, *Mission Impossible*, *Saving Private Ryan*. I think that's because in real life, sometimes taking even simple action is daunting. But please, make a thoughtful, strategic plan and be that action hero.

You will sleep so much better.

Highlights

1. Admit it when you're wrong. Your opinion is less valued and trusted if you can never admit you made a mistake.
2. If something's not feeling right, figure it out and make a decision. The quicker the better and move on!
3. Be proactive! Never ignore the IRS, vendors, or other government entities. But be aware of phone and email scams—remember the IRS will only contact you by mail.

9

The Importance of Consistent Communication

"Stupid human tricks"

COMEDIAN AND *LATE Night* TV show host David Letterman had a segment called "Stupid human tricks." These were quick clips or live onstage stunts by yes, actual humans! It was a popular part of his show and revealed our absolute fascination with what people will attempt—snakes, heights, fire, eating weird things—whatever your imagination can conceive. Now there are whole YouTube channels dedicated to this stuff, but I'll bet you can come up with some real life "stupid human tricks" you've witnessed in the business world from customers, bosses, coworkers, or vendors. I am not immune. I have contributed some thoughtless attempts myself. Have you? I hear your mind whirring, so read on and let me embarrass myself. Hopefully you will pick up some tips on how to avoid similar tricky moments in your business!

I distinctly remember when a crack in the trust between my partner and me began, and it was my fault. We had been hard at work for at least two years. The store had been open eighteen months, and I had a one-year-old son. We had just acquired a big lot of snow skis from a rental company to resell. We knew they needed to be sorted, processed, and priced. But I was tired and it was a pretty Sunday and my wife said, "Come on, let's take the baby to the zoo!" So I did. Now this was before cell phones, so basically I didn't show up, and my partner worked alone that Sunday morning. When I got in on Monday, I explained and he seemed ok, but down deep I knew I had left him hanging and now he was wary about trusting me. It's not an extreme example, but I count this as one of my personal "stupid human tricks." Soon all was forgiven as we jumped back into the long days of work together, but it can be hard to regain trust once there is a crack.

This next example is a more extreme "stupid human trick." One of my employees decided to add a comment on our computer screen's pop-up "notes" about a customer who was bringing back a return. In her profile section he typed in "b*tch," thinking it only showed up on the computer. Nope, it printed out on her receipt. Yes, I got a call from the husband. Yes, I swore I would fire the young employee, but after long discussions with the manager and employee, I did keep him on staff and tried to use this as a teaching moment.

I should have fired him.

Later, he began stealing from me. The pressure of needing employees and the manager persuading me to keep the employee kept me from making a good decision, and I didn't fire him. I didn't listen to my gut or maybe I was just lazy.

Here's another true story about poor follow up and communication, and it happened while I was trying to have good follow up and communication! I would always conduct monthly employee meetings before the stores opened. We decided to meet at one particular location to show off some of the merchandising, etc. This particular store had a goofy front door that would not lock from the inside. So, as a short-term fix that turned into long-term no follow up, when we were closing up, we slid a baseball bat through the door handles to keep the door shut. It would keep customers out while we closed registers. Then, when time to leave, we would set the alarm, remove the bat, exit through the front door, then lock it from the outside. That morning we all show up with donuts and coffee, ready for the meeting, but we can't open the front door. The baseball bat is holding the door closed from the inside! When we finally got in, we discovered that an assistant manager, who had a key, had decided the store would be a great place to have a tryst with his girlfriend, and they'd secured the door with the bat. He didn't realize we were about to have a manager meeting that morning, and they ran out the back door.

I have found that without manager meetings at least once a week and employee meetings once a month, the level of energy from employees seems to fade. Also, my level of trust in them begins to fade. The same thing happens on an individual employee level. If I don't make some sort of effort to personally work with or speak to an employee, their efforts and my trust in their work goes down. And wouldn't you know it—the incidence of stupid human tricks goes up! Regular and frequent meetings seem to keep stupid human tricks to a minimum. In meetings, my main discussion topics are inventory, marketing, people, and operations. (If you own a service company your list might be marketing, people, operations, sales pipeline, and project management.) Some of my best results came from meetings that were led by other employees, or I listed categories and just let the group talk about what they were proud of, what they weren't, what bugged them, and what were some ideas they wanted to try.

But this is a fact. Whenever I *consistently* held meetings and followed up with an action plan, sales and morale always increased. What's the real payoff for you as owner-manager? More money in your pocket, more time off, and peace of mind when you do have time off! Huge! You have implemented good time management and delegation skills, but I like to call them "lifestyle management" skills. It's the payoff for taking all the risk, long hours, and heartache of starting your own gig!

That reminds me of a story Ray Nitchke, NFL Hall of Famer for the Green Bay Packers in the 60s, shared with me. He and some guys were getting a bit rough in a bar in Green Bay. The owner of the bar called The Coach. Yes, Vince Lombardi! "Hey Coach, your guys are tearing my place apart!" Do you think Coach Lombardi wanted this to be part of his "lifestyle"? Lombardi drove from his house to the bar, reamed these guys out, made them pay for the damage and apologize, then kicked them out. Ray said they all left like a pack of puppies with their tails between their legs. Coach Lombardi might have realized he had slacked off on certain topics in the team meetings. I'll bet he didn't again. Consistent communication. Mice will play when the boss is away.

In a study on human behavior, researchers placed signs around a college campus where bicycles were being stolen. The signs showed a pair of eyes and contained the words: "Cycle Thieves, We Are Watching You." There was a sixty-two percent decrease in the number of thefts.[1] There is also the old adage, "When the farmers walk their fields, the crops grow better." Basically, when you care and show it consistently you will have fewer "stupid human tricks."

The profit and loss payoff for consistent communication is everyone feels like they know what's going on. When there are no mysteries, no gossip floating around the organization, it leads to the best ingredient for top line performance––confidence! When employees have confidence, it shows up in all aspects of the business: confidence when dealing with customers, confidence when dealing with vendors, confidence in executing marketing. There's another great insider benefit: confidence when giving and receiving internal feedback.

If a junior executive knows the strategic goal of the organization, they can confidently speak up on issues. The junior executive level is where many molehill problems can be detected before they turn into mountain problems.

I could always tell when my employees lacked confidence because I got more phone calls from them when I wasn't in the store. As the staff or manager grew in experience, they called me less frequently. But I still needed to follow up. There was one instance when I made a poor decision to promote an employee to manager only because he was older and had more seniority. But even after working for me for three years he did not have the confidence to manage even the most minor of management decisions. However, I didn't know this for a few weeks because I wasn't getting any phone calls from him. I'm thinking, *Hey, everything is going smoothly!* But then I started having customers come in and ask me to solve a problem because the manager had told them, "Come back when the owner is here." It was always something minor, like a coupon from another store, a repair, or unusual refund. Something that after three years he should be able to handle. He was so risk-averse he couldn't bring himself to ask another person to do anything, not even accomplish tasks on time. In truth, deep down, I knew despite his age and experience he wasn't the best candidate for the job. I had promoted him thinking, *Hey, he'll step up when he has this responsibility!* I learned an employee needs to perform at the level above them BEFORE being promoted. And now you're asking: How did I extract myself from this bad hire? And what should you do in a similar situation? I'll answer those questions shortly.

Mistakes happen when we're in a hurry. I have a friend who was trained as an emergency medical technician (EMT). I learned a valuable lesson from him: never run. When an EMT shows up to an emergency, they rarely run. They will walk quickly. They will *almost* jog. An EMT will move with a confident purpose. You see, when they show up at a site, they are seen as superheroes. They may not be able to do anything at all for a victim, but they need to exude calm and control in what is often a chaotic situation.

When my dad was on his deathbed with colon cancer at the age of forty-seven, we were alone. It had been quiet for some time. There wasn't much to say but to breathe the same air seemed enough. I got the feeling he wanted to give me some life advice. He looked at me with that wise expression of, "Get ready, this is going to be profound wisdom to carry you through the rest of your life."

My dad said, "Whatever you do, when making decisions, make sure you write it down first and pay attention to what you're doing."

I was a young twenty-five at the time. I just nodded my head, but inside I'm thinking, *What? That's it? That's the profound wisdom?* Over the years, however, I've discovered he was right. Take the time to write down all the options about a decision. Good and bad and in-between. Pay attention to what you're doing. I always took that to mean specific tasks like hammering a nail or driving a car, but running a business and making decisions that affect that business goes on year after year and you can become hypnotized by the road, so to speak. When you snap back to real time in your business you realize, hopefully not too late, your business is headed toward the ditch.

So, what did I do in the case of the longtime employee getting promoted beyond his abilities? Luckily, in our previous reviews, he and I had discussed his strengths and weaknesses in handling uncomfortable situations. When I met with him, I brought up our previous discussions and reviewed his current work effectiveness. In that light he agreed with me and accepted a demotion and a pay decrease. He came back to work the next day a new person—upbeat and positive. He realized he suffocated under responsibility and now he could breathe again! He continued working for me for another year. I was open with the other employees about the leadership change, and they were glad to see it happen because they knew he wasn't the right person for the job. A point to remember—your employees know the mood and abilities of their coworkers better than you.

There are many different styles and methods of communicating within an organization. So get out your test tubes and concoct one that fits your business. It doesn't really matter except make it clear and consistent. Sometimes you'll feel like you're trying to push a wet string uphill, but the goal is to keep the "stupid human tricks" on YouTube and out of your business!

Highlights

1. Write it down and pay attention to what you're doing.
2. Set consistent meetings and training schedules.
3. Don't run all the meetings yourself. Allow staff to plan and organize.
4. The best learning time for you and your employee is the personal debriefing you conduct with an employee to whom you've given responsibility.

10

Staff Training, Expectations, and Attitude

It's not the millennials!

AS I'VE MENTIONED, my franchise business just happened to be a local sporting goods retailer, a national brand franchise that became a piece of the community's fabric. It gave me a day-to-day, true grassroots perspective of a diverse population—diversity of income, age, religion, education, drug use, morals, you name it, at some point I've seen it walk through the door. It's an open door dealing with the public. But one of the most revealing aspects of diversity I observed is the diversity of attitude. No matter your generation or whether you're an owner or employee, I've seen attitude make you or break you. Every generation has had friction with the generation replacing it, such as the flappers in the early 1920s, the James Dean "rebels without a cause" in the '50s, and the "hippies are destroying America" in the '70s. Today, people complain about millennials, but I can tell you, it's not the millennials.

To maintain a productive workforce in today's marketplace, you need to be aware of the factors that affect the attitude of employees, customers, and owners. One of the biggest influences is the health of personal household budgets. Do you know what most affects the attitude Americans have toward their personal budget? The price of a gallon of gas. This was published in a working paper from the Bureau of Economic Research, "Mental Accounting and Gasoline Consumption," that said, "Households adjusted their mix of gasoline purchases almost twenty times more to a reduction in their buying power because of an increase in gasoline prices than to an equivalent reduction in income from other sources." [1]

You know how we joke about the government spending thousands and thousands of dollars and years of effort on a study to figure out what we already know? This is one of those times.

I figured this out from listening to my customers every day and actually observing them making their mental spending calculations. From 1991 through 2018, every time the price of gas spiked, people hunkered down and got stingy with their spending. It really hits people in their daily cash flow, and it really affects their attitude. It was also a harbinger for the economy. My business always weathered it, usually by my working harder and sometimes smarter. Attitude affects motivation, and sometimes we need a kick in the attitude!

In recent years many business owners complain of having a difficult time finding young executives who can learn and embody the culture. The catchall phrase is, "Those millennials! They just don't want to work!" I totally disagree with that. It is now known that there are two categories of millennials: The ones who bust their tails and the ones who fail to launch. And one group pisses off the other because that group makes them look bad.[2] For the group we complain about, I would propose it is not their fault. After all, we caved in and bought them the $100 sneakers, latest iPhones, big-screen TVs for their bedroom, ad infinitum. As they grew to the age of majority we told them, "Oh, you're not mature enough to drink, yet you are mature enough to drink if you join the military. Oh, you're not mature enough to own a pistol, yet you can if you're in the military. Oh, you're not mature enough to rent a car until you're twenty-five." They also can't rent a condo or trade certain stocks or many other examples of age maturity restraints and discrimination. WE, as a society, have told these young adults "you can't do these things." So they don't. They live in the basement. And why can people in the military legally have responsibilities their peers are denied when they are eighteen? I would submit it's because of proper training. And I submit that the other age issues also boil down to training.

So how does this relate to a business? Businesses sometimes fall into this same line of thinking, even if you own a franchise, and you're going by all the guidelines. Examine your business. Has it fallen into a culture of "We better not try that. We're not ready"? Or maybe it's bogged down with systems and procedures and traditional personnel reviews that hold employees back? Once held back or told they're not ready for a project, those employees are more reluctant to step up with ideas. In other words, they mentally "just go live in the basement."

So don't always blame the workforce. Take a good look in the mirror. Ask yourself: "What in my organization am I completely happy and comfortable with? What part do I feel like I constantly struggle with? Does my millennial, Gen -X, or boomer self need to be trained? Do I need to kick myself out of my own basement? Is there someone on my staff I can reach out to today and help their attitude?" Getting in the habit of looking for these attitude-adjustment moments has a huge positive impact for your organization. Then it becomes a way of life. You are helping, and you may not even know it. I call it attitude training.

Customers want to connect with the owner of a local business. And I love it! They'll always ask, "How's business?" And whether it's a guy working for the city or a CEO of a big company, I would get a knowing smile when I answered, "Business is great. When I work. Not so great when I don't." Immediately, the customer understands my attitude. I do relay it in a fun, lighthearted way, but I also want my employees to hear this! I want my employees to know I'm paying attention to who's working, and I expect hard work of myself too.

As humans it is perfectly normal to get complacent during good times. Things are going well and we relax. We take our eye off the ball. In business, there is always something that comes along that snaps your attention back on target. Something like a 2000 tech-bubble crash or political blowups around the world that screw up your supply chain. People forget about the dockworker strike in Los Angeles right before Christmas in 2012. That strike hurt our sales in Atlanta, and we had to scramble for product. You realize you have to go back to doing your chores. Stay focused, get your attitude right.

A big part of the satisfaction of owning your own business or franchise is you get to interact with your neighbors every day. For twenty-eight years, I got to witness parents "training" their kids. Every week, if not every day, in our store there would be an instance where a child, usually middle school-aged but sometimes younger, would shop with their parents. They would need something of utility, maybe an equipment bag or bat or soccer ball and especially cleats. After looking and looking, I would find several items that solved the problem. Yet the child would protest about color or style or something entirely irrelevant. The youngster wanted the new one for $80 or $100 when we had perfect used items for $6. Often the parent would cave in to the kid's demands. Many times I could tell if the family was well-off or not. At some point, I would look the kid in the eye and ask them, "Hey, you know what my dad used to tell me?" Blank stare. The child didn't care but I told him anyway. My dad would say, "That's ok, you don't have to play baseball. There's a list of chores to do at home. Let's go." The look on their face at first was, "Oh, this guy is pulling my leg." But I just held their gaze for a moment, hoping a sense of personal humility and pride in helping out one's family was planted. There are many images planted in our brains about far-reaching consequences—the butterfly that flutters its wings and causes vibrations to build into a storm on the other side of the world. A pebble thrown into a pond causes rings that spread beyond our sight. In other words, something small can leave a lasting impression.

I lived my own example of this. I am an only child, and my parents were divorced when I was thirteen. We moved 500 miles and eight hours away from my dad. My mom and I moved in with my grandmother in a tiny town in central Florida. I knew no one. The difference from suburban Atlanta to cowboy country central Florida was significant. One of my mom's friends in Florida, a man she'd known since high school, recognized I was a boy trying to become a man. A boy who, for daily purposes, had lost his father. My mom's friend invited me to go dove hunting on his property. I was ecstatic. I remember that afternoon as clear as a Florida spring's water—riding in his small Datsun truck, bouncing through the cow pasture to set up, shooting doves with his 20-gauge shotgun. Together, we cleaned what we shot then went inside and had lunch. I felt so special. I was a man and could do "man" things. The confidence boost for a thirteen year old can't be described. Thirty years later I went back to that little town for my grandmother's funeral, and I saw him standing by the gravesite with other friends of the family. I approached him and introduced myself. He did not recognize me. I reminded him of that day and thanked him profusely—told him how much it meant to me—that one day shooting doves out in his cow pasture. He had absolutely no recollection of the event. He was slightly amazed at himself, I think. I think maybe to him it was just an ordinary thoughtful deed—as natural as holding the door open for someone. He did not realize he was my pebble in the pond at that moment in my life.

Now in the business of sales and service we call this moment "the cherry." The something special you do at the end of a transaction to create a lasting impression in the customer's mind. Chick-fil-A ends a transaction with the associate saying, "My pleasure." UPS and the US Postal Service now allow their drivers to give a dog biscuit to dogs on their route. Publix carries your groceries to your car. Those touches are ever so special. In my business I trained my staff to look for opportunities to compliment or point out something special to the customer. Things like, "Hey, cool shoes!" or "Nice car!" We had a "Big Orange Bell" we would ring for just about any occasion but especially if it was someone's first time in the store. Compliment the kids on their neat T-shirt, carry things to the car even if they are not bulky, give the customer extra ideas on saving money, and we tried to always have cross-marketing materials from other local businesses so we could give customers coupons to the barbershop or restaurant down the street. The "cherry" moment is an awesome place for creativity among staff too. These were my "cherry" moments—when I saw an employee initiate something like this on their own. But I had to push constantly to train this into our associates' habits and our corporate culture. Will you?

So it's not the millennials. It's us. It's how we train. There have been some studies on how bad attitudes show up due to low emotional intelligence.[3] Our employees have lots of information, and they're not dumb. They just haven't endured the experiences to develop the emotional wherewithal to cope. As parents, we may have tried to keep our kids "happy" all the time. As a boss, I would sometimes slide into this trap of trying to keep my employees "happy." But kids AND employees have to experience uncomfortable situations to grow and handle the future responsibilities you want to delegate. Remember, delegating translates into good "time management," which translates into great "lifestyle management" for you. So pushing your millennial staff to learn from difficult situations and experiences is important. We franchisees are going to go through tons of employees, and it is not our job to keep them happy. In fact, sometimes we try to keep everyone happy in our business to the detriment of overall morale. Training using face-to-face role-playing has helped me in this regard. I used this model to train new employees, especially on how to deal with unhappy customers. It was also fun for group meetings, where I let more experienced employees play the role of unhappy customer. The experienced employee would come up with all kinds of scenarios to stump the newer employees. It was fun and engaging for all the employees!

For younger employees who seemed to enjoy job-hopping, I had better retention when I created a job path that moved them from role to role every two months. Basically, I had them job-hopping within the company. This is exactly the model IBM and GE developed early on—keep your staff learning. You know what? It never ends. We're constantly developing our workforce for better results. It's most important to keep yourself motivated with a good attitude. Keep it fresh for yourself so you can keep it fresh for your employees!

Keeping your business-self fresh is just like working out. It's challenging to be consistent, but there are several ways I did it, and you can too. Join local networking groups like the Rotary International and local chambers of commerce, which attract a variety of business professionals. Attend national conferences, including some focused on your industry, but once in a while go to one in an ancillary industry. For example: Do you have a pool business? Attend a concrete or water industry group meeting. Construction or real estate? Attend environmental or forestry events. Sporting goods? Attend plastics or medical research conferences. You just never know what cross-networking ideas might pop up. So right now, today, put it on the list! Here's to your great attitude! Oh, and by the way—you'll meet a ton of millennials who are kicking butt!

Highlights

1. Train yourself and your employees every day on how to deliver the "cherry on top." Exceed expectations!
2. Look for opportunities to keep your own attitude fresh and curious.
3. Whatever happens, don't blame others.

11

Establish Good Business Practices

Then choose when to be a "disrupter"

THE FAMOUS LINE the pirate belts out in *Pirates of the Caribbean* about "parlaying" gives the person temporary protection from the brutal treatment of the bad guys. They refer to this "pirate code" that can never be broken several times early in the movie, until the point where a "parlay" is decidedly not in their best interest. That's when one famously yells that the "pirate code is really more of a 'guideline.'" Does this sound familiar when it comes to your best business practices? We are now at a point in business history where the word "disrupt" is in vogue. It's another way of saying, "We're breaking the old business practices down. We break the rules and make our own." You're a cool, edgy, forward-thinking business owner and influencer if you are a "disrupter."

I've got news for you—business practices have been "disrupted" for centuries. Genghis Khan was a "disrupter." Thomas Edison was a "disrupter." The railroad barons and oil titans were disrupters. Ted Turner, Richard Branson, Steve Jobs, too. Some people "disrupt" just for the sake of being an outlier. Some do it with a strategic, pinpoint-focused plan that is measurable, which means accountable to a timetable. Who do you think is more successful? The outlier disrupter or the strategic disrupter? Disrupters have to be even more disciplined in maintaining solid principled practices.

One of the coolest rainbow moments of owning your business or franchise is realizing you are becoming your own disrupter by stepping outside the norm of how people perceive *you*. You are taking control of *your* life on *your* terms, and it can be quite disrupting. It can and will disrupt your home and lifestyle rhythm. It can and will affect your take-home pay and cash flow.

These two things alone will cause stress for you and your family. If it were easy everyone would do it. The big, deep breaths of satisfaction when you see the results of your work and effort and the freedom to make decisions without deferring to anyone else are fantastic! To be the last one to leave, turn the key in the lock, walk out to your car in the lot, and look up at the sign with *your* business's name on it is a glorious moment. An even deeper satisfaction occurs when you realize your idea and hard work are generating revenue to support all the households of the people on your staff. Oh, yeah! Deep satisfaction. We go into business to make money and become financially secure, but the gravy of these other benefits sometimes can't be measured. Those benefits are there, and you will have so many of those moments.

So how do you go from being Superman to feeling like one of the Three Stooges in less than an hour? I came in early one morning wearing a coat and tie because I had to attend a funeral a few hours later. I discovered we had to pick up and deliver a treadmill that morning and one employee had injured his knee in Brazilian jiu jitsu training and the other employee doubted their own ability. So I peeled off the coat, tie, and dress shirt, Superman style, then backed up the great balls of fire pickup truck, loaded the new treadmill and off we went! Upon arriving we saw this home had a steep downhill driveway leading to the backyard basement. Pavement turned to cobblestones turned to gravel turned to a slope covered with leaves and weeds leading to a set of narrow wooden stairs with one missing stairstep. The owner had "thoughtfully" placed a two by six, eight-foot board for us to "walk the plank" over the stairs. Presumably, we would walk-balance-slide this two-hundred-pound treadmill, plus ourselves, across the six-inch swaying, sagging piece of "help." In my head, I could hear The Three Stooges: Larry, Curly, and Moe, approaching. Things could get out of control. We removed the plank. Thanks! We were then escorted into the basement and threaded our way around several workshop benches, clusters of filing cabinets, and some numerous piles of undefinable stuff. Other piles had nice table lamps, without shades, balanced on top. There were piles of pottery shards, and items that looked like materials for summer camp art class. For some reason, none of us wanted to inquire about the half-dozen five-gallon glass carboy containers filled with water and covered with dust. *How long had they been there?* Finally, we came upon a workout space crammed with lots of exercise items collected over what seemed to be a thirty-year period. Can you say, "As seen on TV"? Yes, there was a Thighmaster.

"Here she is!"

Remember the pirate and sailor stories where the pirate spends all his time building a ship inside a bottle? That's our owner and his treadmill. It had been brought into the basement in a box and constructed there. It appeared to never have been used. I call those exercise sculptures—you set it up and stare at it. Well, to remove it, we needed to partially disassemble it. So, we're staring at this thing, and I could feel the humidity percolating. Did I fail to mention it was Georgia in July? Did I fail to mention I was wearing dress slacks and dress shoes? Maybe we can remove the treadmill in one piece? It's a million-to-one chance but we've got a chance! *Crap. It's not going to work.* The inside door was wider than the outside door. So we stared at the beast for a minute. It was decided we had to take off its giant, oversized, plastic monitor head. We asked to borrow an Allen wrench and Phillips-head screwdriver. After assuming the facial expressions of surgeons, we began to remove screws and more screws and two more. The big plastic beast's monitor head was loose but not coming off. I looked at my manager and he looked at me. All I had to say was "one, two, three," and we busted that piece-of-crap plastic right off the treadmill. Then it came out easy. I was sure glad my town recycled large appliances!

When your entire staff is stumped on a project, you have to lead. Problems and timetables are surmountable. By strategically doing work that may be technically below your pay grade, you set a great example for the rest of the company. So be ready to rip off that suit, Superman, and get dirty! When employees see you demonstrate your best business skills, they learn best business practices. Be your own disrupter. Be the pirate and parlay on your own terms—just do it with character, honesty, and discipline!

Highlights

1. Surprise your staff. When they're struggling, don't be afraid to dive in and help them manage a project.
2. Give your staff all the credit.

12

Good People...and Others

*The value of your amazing (and odd) community,
customers, and relationships*

"GOOD PEOPLE." WHEN we hear this phrase, we think we know what it means. When I interviewed a potential employee, I would attempt to impress upon them what "good people" means to me, how I expected them to conduct themselves, and what they could expect to see in other people. To do that, I told them this story.

There is a multimillionaire in an office on Wall Street who is as honest as the day is long. He has a coworker next door who will say and do anything to squeeze a dollar from a trusting client. Thirty stories below is a homeless person sitting on the sidewalk who will return a $20 bill to the passerby who dropped it. He is sitting next to another homeless person who is looking for any opportunity to steal. Morals, ethics, and integrity aren't indicated by attire or address.

There are many studies confirming that people will work for less pay as long as they know they are doing "good," and their work has meaning and makes an impact. As evidence, see the *Harvard Business Review* article, "9 out of 10 People are Willing to Earn Less Money to Do More-Meaningful Work," November 6, 2018.[1] On those days when everything seems to be going in a ditch, think about the ways you're getting paid that don't show up in your bank account. Here are some examples of how I got paid and ultimately confirmed the mission of my business.

One night a man and his son came in the store to return a brand-new baseball glove that was defective. He had a game the next day, of course, so I told them to go over and pick out any glove they wanted, new or used, and it would be no charge. The look of relief and thrill on their faces was uplifting. I would like to think they remember the moment as fondly as I do.

Then there was Louie, who was perhaps in his eighties. Louie was a little bent over and always wore a hat and a sweater vest. He had the sweetest demeanor, a great smile, and he knew his business. He purchased rope scraps at a discount and used them to make hammocks by hand. He crafted the wooden end pieces and tied the knots and wove the rope himself. The hammocks looked like Pawley's Island hammocks but were made so much better. Louie would bring me four or five at a time and put them on consignment. Then I didn't see him for a while. One day a woman came in to pick up his money. She was his wife, whom I had never met. She told me Louie had died. I have one of Louie's hammocks in my back yard. Louie is not dead.

Rick was a police officer for a small suburban city nearby. He grew up in "Philly" and was a bit rough around the edges but had a soft, easy-going manner. I always got the sense his life had been a struggle. Rick loved hockey and played goalie in a men's league. Goalies get a little beat up. He always brought in items to trade or buy, scrapping for gear on a limited budget but sacrificing to play. When I met him, he was in his forties and not married, but eventually he did marry. I got to meet his wife. She was his pride and joy, and when they had a son, Rick really blossomed. His boy was going to play hockey. For at least ten years or more Rick came in the store on a regular basis. Then one day he came in and said he'd gotten a divorce. I don't remember Rick coming in much more after that. I miss Rick.

There was a little girl who came in with her daddy to buy her first softball glove. They looked and looked. Finally, after finding just the right one, she asked if she could write her name in the glove after they bought it. But then she looked at the glove and exclaimed, almost in tears, "Someone else has already written their name in it, Daddy!" We saw it was Dale Murphy, a former Atlanta Brave. It was the preprinted signature that comes in all the gloves these days. The father and I looked at each other and split a gut laughing! He'll tell that story at her wedding one day.

In the early years, we were open from 10 a.m. until 9 p.m. I remember one day when we had made barely any sales, and for the last couple of hours I was there by myself. There were bills to pay that week, and the pressure was building. Feeling a bit depressed, I considered closing early. Right before closing, a young couple came in and bought a three-hundred-pound Olympic weight set and bench combo that doubled the day's sales. They were so thankful I was still open. Their son's birthday was the next day, and they worked late jobs too. What a relief for all of us!

Renee was a small, wiry guy about eighty years old who drove a beat-up Ford Explorer filled with odds and ends. He would buy from thrift stores and resell to us. We had many customers like Renee who provided a wonderful symbiotic service—they brought us products we didn't have time to seek, and we provided them with supplemental income. We helped teach these folks about what to look for and how to assess items, but Renee always had a tough time. He would bring in equipment we could never sell because it was out of date, ugly, or broken, and he would be so disappointed because he was trying so hard. Sometimes, I'd buy a few of his items, then throw them out or donate them. But Renee was a thinker and an inspiration. He constantly preached to my staff, telling them they had unused talents, and they should read books about great people. He sat with me for hours, giving advice on topics ranging from business to starting a nonprofit for prostate cancer patients. Renee held two records in the *Guinness World Book of Records*, and he had coached alongside the famous John Wooden of UCLA. Renee took the first American baseball team to play exhibition baseball in Europe. He had stories and newspaper clippings as proof, but he never bragged. Instead, he used these experiences to prod and teach others. To show, "Hey! See what a wiry, beat-up old man in a beat-up old truck can do?" I love that guy. I will always keep learning because of Renee!

Then there was Dave. Dave was a state champion golf and tennis player in high school and college. He came in every week on Tuesdays, like a clock. He even started helping to arrange things in the golf section on his own. Dave taught me more about golf and tennis than anyone else. It goes to show that you don't have to be *the* expert. Just get better at being *an* expert. I used Dave as an example to many employees to show how if you just shut up and listen to a customer you can learn so much. Ask questions and a customer will teach you many aspects of your own product or service. What a great guy!

There was the man who stopped in on his way to Florida from Canada every year. The man, who had homes in both places, would gather used sports equipment and sell them on consignment through us to raise money for local charities in Atlanta. All because his daughter lived in Atlanta.

Herb was another retired gentleman that brought us great loads of used baseball gloves. He was the Energizer Bunny. Loved to play golf with his buddies after he quit his union job as a machinist.

And if relationships are what real business is all about, then always keep the tellers at the bank on your side! Bill, a retired minister, taught that as well. Pro players and their families from the NFL, MLB, NBA, and more. The rodeo bull rider who got engaged, and he sold his spurs, rope, and saddle because his fiancé didn't want him to ride anymore. The divorced wife of a WWE wrestler who sold his tights and patent leather lace-up boots. The everyday golf traders. Hal, Bill, John, and a dozen more who worked on golf clubs in the home shops. John, the injured UPS driver. State senators, mayors, US congressmen. People who knew the town when it had more cotton fields than red lights.

And like every gray scale of humanity, there are the people who have not found their goodness.

There was a man who went in the bathroom with a bunch of clothes and put every one of them on under his regular clothes. It was obvious and it was not pretty. We called the police but did not press charges. He needed other help.

There was the shoplifter dressed in a suit and tie who stole disc golf items.

There was an employee who taught another employee how to steal.

The drunk guy in a polo shirt and khakis riding off with a bicycle. An elderly couple who drove off with the wrong (and more expensive) product and when we called them to switch it for the correct one, they refused. They even admitted that what they were doing was dishonest but blamed us. And then wouldn't pay the difference. Well, I guess you shine your own halo.

Crackheads, meth heads, and an employee whose personality was the combination of the books *Blink* and *The Sociopath Next Door*. There was a mom, grand mom, and kids who were selling the dad's golf bag. We found an old bottle of Jack Daniels in it, and I had to swear to that to the woman's lawyer. I think the dad had a court order to stop drinking. I kind of felt sorry for him because that bottle could have been there for years. Dependency people are like squirrels. They can hide a lot of nuts and forget where most of them are hidden.

Weirdest thing found in a golf bag? False teeth. We had a running contest for this but nothing could ever beat false teeth.

And wow, there were so many opportunities to make an immediate difference in people's lives right in our neighborhood! Charities, if we gave to one, we gave to a thousand.

A cook at a Mexican restaurant had his bike stolen. We gave him a new one.

I hired lots of young people from drug dependency programs.

I hired a convicted felon, a former drug dealer from Chicago, who decided to head south before he was killed on the streets. He eventually became my manager.

I hired a fifty-four-year-old convicted murderer. He'd served thirty-five years for killing a baby he was babysitting when he was seventeen. He was high, and the baby wouldn't stop crying, so he shook it to death. When he got out of prison, no one would give him a chance. He broke down in tears when I told him he was hired.

We provided a place for brain-injured persons to rehab and do meaningful work.

With any business—small, large, service, manufacturing, or retail—you encounter the good people and the not-so-good people. Try to stay curious, be interested in their personal well being, and learn from all of them. Even the rudest person or client can sometimes provide a future asset, and ultimately that is what business is about—building an asset that you can sell.

Many of your best assets are sometimes the people just standing along the wall at the dance waiting for someone to ask them. In the Scouts, the Wood Badge program gives current leaders the tools to "train the trainers." In other words, learn how to get all the other parents trained to volunteer and help out. A key part is making sure you pick your head up at a meeting to see which parents are attending but seem to just hang out. In your business and community, I guarantee there are folks just doing their job and kind of "hanging out along the wall of the dance." But once you've engaged that employee or vendor in some personal, get-to-know-you conversation, they may be willing to do more and have a better attitude. This is a business lesson that cannot be measured.

This is your small business or franchise, and like it or not, when you opened the doors you became a part of the community. Go ahead and embrace it. Give your community a hug. It's a good habit. And habits carry over. Can I get an amen?

Highlights

1. Pay attention—the value of your business endeavor is increased by the little things—just like the movie, *It's a Wonderful Life*.

13

Lessons on Expansion

Hey, y'all, watch this!

"HEY, Y'ALL, WATCH this" and "oops" are some of the most famous last words ever spoken. So, let's finish the sentence. Famous last words ever spoken before what? Before trying that backflip with the bicycle? Before jumping in the creek from the rope swing? Before lighting that birthday drink on fire, then drinking it? Or just expanding a company and taking on loads of debt?

I think I tried just about all of those, but none are seared into my memory as well as the "expanding a company and taking on loads of debt." I should have yelled out, "Hey, y'all, watch this!" This story isn't about cash flow, but how I recovered my business and went on to ultimate success.

My plan was reasonable when I bought my first franchise. Open eight to ten stores in ten years, then sell them. Go on and start another business. My partner and I opened two in two years, and they were growing nicely. Two years later he wanted to leave the business, and we parted amicably. Two years later, I felt like I had a good handle on operating multiple stores and decided to "make my move." I opened a third store, and two years after that opened a fourth store. But I also relocated two other stores at the same time. Opening stores and moving stores takes cash. Again, I thought I had planned well, but I soon realized operating four stores takes more cash per individual location and the same expanded management infrastructure as literally operating ten stores. I had not planned on that. Why? Because I didn't know.

This is actually another good test of a good franchisor. A good one will not let you expand until you run through all the five-year P&L and cash flow projections properly. The current franchisor does require this now but didn't require me to do it early on. I paid the price.

I felt like I'd let The Three Stooges into my business. Within ninety days, tight cash flow was killing me because growing existing locations became exacerbated by moving the other locations. (Always plan for at least a ten percent decrease in store sales after moving.) Something else I didn't know— every time we relocated a store, even if it was within the same strip mall, we saw a decrease in business as customers figured out that we had moved. We even had big signs in the windows saying where we'd moved to, and people *still* thought we'd gone out of business. Quickly, every little issue within your operation is magnified. Employee problems on top of the extra cash needed and the slowdown in sales combined to create inventory control and supply issues, which put even more strain on cash flow. You can see how a spiral out of control can begin.

As I've mentioned, it took me eight years to build a great business, and it took me two to swamp it. After eighteen months I realized my dilemma. We owed vendors, rent, state and federal taxes, advertisers. We owed everybody. The business owed $185,225, all of it overdue. These are real numbers of accounts payable overdue for just two of the stores. This $185,225 was our short-term overdue debt from two of the stores that together grossed less than two million a year and gross netted ten percent of that. So, our short-term debt was approximately the same as our one-year net profit. Out of that net profit we still had to pay long-term debt service. The percentages were not good, but I recognized it fairly early. Historically, in big company fiascos, the pain just keeps getting dragged out for years because everyone in the giant organization keeps thinking someone else is working on the problem (see Sears, Toys "R" Us, and Sports Authority). Problems and the responsibility for their resolution are spread and shared throughout a large organization so issues don't seem so personally dire. Well, in a small business it's personally dire. If the CEO of Sears, Sports Authority, or Toys "R" Us had to take their personal credit card to get a cash advance to make payroll, perhaps their companies and employees and stock holders wouldn't have lost and suffered as much. Still, my percentages were better than Sports Authority's when it tanked. They had gross revenues of $2.7 billion and debt equaling a billion, so more than thirty percent debt to their gross revenue before expenses. If anyone in the boardroom yelled, "Hey, y'all, watch this," no one heard it. As a franchisee, it is easy to get caught up in the excitement of seeing other franchisees grow, and that's good when used as a motivator. But please make sure you balance the gung ho optimism with the reality that your balance sheet may be different than that other franchisee's. That's what happened to me. I tried to grow too fast and acquired too much debt for my owner-manager skill set. Your owner-manager skill set may also be different.

So how do you not get caught in this type of problem? And how do you get yourself out? First, set yourself some rules of the road—balance sheet and P&L rules of the road. For example, make sure your three biggest expenses are maintained at a set percentage of gross revenue. In my business it meant rent and payroll should stay at ten percent or less of gross revenue and advertising at three percent. I use this as an example, but depending on your industry you should have a number that works. When you see your monthly expenses creeping past what you've planned, there better be a good, strategically planned reason or take action now! Not next quarter, not next month. NOW! You have four options—mark up inventory and services and improve margins, mark down inventory and services for a surge of cash flow at reduced profit, cut expenses, or do a little bit of all three. As I mentioned before, I survived three economic hiccups. We started during the first recession, dumb luck!

The second downturn was the tech bubble in 2000. That just happened to coincide with my decision to grow too fast, which caused my almost-going-out-of-business sale. To survive, I initiated these dramatic actions: I closed a store, parted with a partner on a store, and sold a store. Results! The sold store paid a good portion of debt. The closed store stopped the bleeding. The partnership separation allowed me to focus like a laser on the remaining store—to ramp it up and give it the attention that created cash flow, which in turn justified to the bank a refinance plan that rolled the rest of the short-term debt into long-term debt, and becoming crazy-fun profitable again!

The third economic hiccup, you might call it more of a stroke, was the great recession of 2008. And what do you know? I didn't panic. Even though during the first four months of the year, which was our busiest time of the year, our sales dropped twenty-five percent. So I implemented all my aforementioned options, plus one more. I cut my general expenses, trimmed payroll slightly, renegotiated our lease to a lower rate, raised some prices, cut prices on slow-moving items, and—wait for it—tripled my advertising budget! Another great example of turning a dead end into a cul-de-sac!

By the end of the year we had fully recovered and matched the previous year's revenue but with increased margins. I also created a big team-training effort for employees. We trained on the customer experience. We trained on add-on sales. We remerchandised the store. We trained on product information. We said "yes!" to some new categories we'd shied away from. We got tight as a team. And it worked!

Traditional wisdom in retail says, when marking down and discounting merchandise, you always take your biggest markdown first. Don't creep into it. It's exactly the same when you realize your ship has bumped into an iceberg. Don't wait for the orchestra to start playing on the foredeck. Make changes quickly and with confidence. Employees will follow with confidence, even if the operational situation is uncomfortable in the short-term.

Now this was a tiny, tiny store, and the numbers don't impress, but baseball is catch, throw, hit. In other words, it's all fundamentals. All of my four stores were profitable. I just couldn't continue to operate the business with the lack of human resource infrastructure and low cash flow I put myself into. Yes, my ego cried out to take on more debt and keep pushing, but I returned to profitability faster by stepping back quickly and refocusing. Sears might have been Walmart and Amazon rolled into one, if it had reacted a lot quicker.

I paid off every single entity we ever owed money to. I got a great education on how to work with our departments of revenue. All of it gave me even more and better standing with my creditors and vendors. They all knew I stood by my sacred word and honor. I am personally invested in my community too—I had to look people in the eye. Maybe if more corporate executives were forced to get local, they wouldn't be able to "escape" through corporate transfer or Chapter 11.

I look back on this time as one of my biggest accomplishments in life—knowing how close I was to the brink, bringing it all back to profitability, and eventually laying out a five-year plan to sell the business that I executed perfectly. That's when I actually leaned out of the car window while driving down the interstate and yelled, "Hey, y'all, watch this!"

You can do it too!

Highlights

1. If you find yourself in a dire situation, cut back until the point you have control again.
2. Don't go to sleep at the wheel while growing too fast. Stay awake!
3. I finally put my previous lessons into action. Get a mentor, make quick decisions, institute consistent training and meetings, communicate with vendors and bankers, and advertise consistently. You should do these things from day one!

14

Business is Like A Marriage

Stay committed, stay motivated

IT IS AMAZING how similar owning a business is to a marriage. It's a relationship thing. Kind of like how similar raising a dog is to raising children. Yes, dogs just want to be near you. Share time with you. Learn new tricks from you. Whether they know it or show it, they definitely want to be touched and soothed by you. They want your attention. They need your attention. Now replace the word "they" with "child." Now try "spouse." Now insert the word "business."

Now some people adopt a dog or get married or have children for all the wrong reasons. They are bored. They are trying to keep up with the "Joneses." They are pressured by someone else's agenda. Perhaps they're running away from something else in their life. They think having a dog, child, spouse, business, fill in the blank, will fix it all. Now everything will be all right.

Examine yourself. Are you going into business for the right reasons? If you're not sure, don't worry! You haven't screwed up. Hopefully these stories of how I earned my scabs and scars will help you refocus your motivations. Discovering the right reasons to go into business is an amazing inspirational motivator! It will be the energy that keeps you going in a positive direction when business gets tough. I'm not trying to scare you off. I'm just pointing out some things I've observed in twenty-eight years of business and thirty-two years of marriage. So how did I stay committed? How did I know when I should plan for the eventual sale or business succession plan? Read on!

While attending our yearly national franchisee conferences, I was constantly amazed at how often I would meet a business owner who was struggling. I'd ask them about their marketing efforts, the reports they used, their employee incentives, and almost always they brushed off my questions, saying, "Nothing I do works. The marketing materials provided to us are not right for me." Excuses rolled off. Almost one hundred percent of the complaining owners didn't have a consistent plan or budget, and if they did make one, they didn't execute. So, this person risked their entire future, career, savings, family security, and in many instances their home, to go into business. They're risking and spending several hundred thousand dollars or more, and they won't execute a basic marketing plan and spend $500 or $1,000 a month on marketing. Somehow, they've gotten comfortable being mediocre. They have just enough success to survive but are still struggling so they complain. Somehow, they are not motivated to improve.

Boggles the mind.

Every franchisor has this type of franchisee. I know fellow business owners from around town and around the country who are struggling. Perhaps they've just bought their business or they've been in business for twenty years. Yet I don't see them at our national conferences. If I am going into surgery and my doctor has twenty years of experience, I'm feeling pretty good and confident he is capable to do the job. But if right before they put me to sleep I hear the nurse whisper to the anesthesiologist, "This surgeon hasn't learned anything new in fifteen years," I'd get a bit nervous. In fact, I'd be running down the hall with my booty showing out of my gown!

I don't care what you sell—if you are not constantly working to become a better professional, standing still means you're losing ground. The scout leaders I've worked with call it "constantly sharpening the knife." Can I get a little bit mentally and professionally sharper?

So again, this person has risked everything in their career, future earnings, savings, family stability, to open this business, and they won't spend $1,500 twice a year to get out and learn new things. They are not motivated to improve. Or maybe they're frozen in place and can't make a decision. Like when I was in the camping shelter listening to mice in the dark!

Boggles the mind!

Sometimes, motivating yourself occurs by motivating the staff. I always see two images of motivational leadership stereotypes: The gung ho *Braveheart*-style warrior holding a banner, running into the flames and fire of battle, and the general sitting behind the lines on horseback or jeep, monitoring communications, issuing orders. Depending on the story, the leader may be calm and cool and confident or panicked and frustrated and blundering.

There is a time for warriors and a time for generals. How does one know which leadership style to choose? That's the classic leadership question every baseball coach asks: When do I rush out on the field and kick dirt on the umpire's shoes?

There always seem to be some forces that are trying to wear you down. Like baseball legend Casey Stengel said, "The trick to managing a ball club is to keep the five guys who hate you away from the other four who haven't made up their minds." That's the way a business feels at times.

Even though I'm a mostly positive person, I'm also more emotional. My friends told me to take some "asshole lessons" because there are times you need to pull out a can of "whoop-ass" when everyone is looking for you to save the day. Thanks to my friends, I've learned to be more strategic.

In the Academy Award-winning movie *All That Jazz* about Broadway great Bob Fosse, you see his morning ritual in a fast-paced, quickly edited montage. He is groaning with aches and a hangover. He is popping pills, showering, applying lotions, stretching, eye drops—the works. It's like renovating and jump-starting a broken-down pickup truck every day. But in the very last shot he is staring into the mirror like a god. He has a huge smile on his face, and he says to the mirror, "It's showtime!" He was bringing his can of "whoop-ass" to work every day.

I find by keeping a generally positive outlook and projecting that out into the store environment it helps the employees and the customers. But then there are times when my energy drops, and it is a monumental effort to walk out on that "stage" and project positivity when I really just want to crawl back under the covers. If a customer or employee projects their positive outlook or spirit upon me, that positive energy is like a kick in the pants. I truly believe if I didn't push myself to continually look for the bright side and push people in a positive direction, their energy would not be there to lift me up when I need it. Think of it as a boomerang effect, if you will.

Wow! Boggles the mind!

Ever notice how the word "morale" is rarely used except in the case of "bad morale"? Or "We need to improve morale." Bad morale is the elephant in the room no one wishes to address. It is the ongoing soap opera in your office. Sometimes gossip and employee friction are going on, and you as a leader don't know it, especially as it relates to social media and posting. Literally within hours of a new hire coming on board, all the employees are sharing or texting. I found one way of addressing both the issue of morale and employee friction is to set a goal for the business, track it on a daily basis, then reward the whole staff with a dinner, a trip to the ball game, or a night out at an arcade.

Staying motivated for the long haul means keeping your eye on the final goal, which is selling your business or passing it on. In the beginning, it's hard to anticipate that far ahead. So the phrase "til death do us part" takes on an interesting meaning. That phrase is the one big difference between a business and a marriage, especially if you are involved in a partnership. So in business, I guess we should say "til divorce do us part." When you organize your business partnership, you should also organize and plan for a divorce. When my first partner and I organized our S corporation we made sure it was split legally, fifty-one percent   to forty-nine percent. Even though in daily operations we operated as a fifty-fifty split and shared decisions equally, I owned fifty-one percent. This legal share designation gave one person the power to force a decision, if needed. We never needed to go there, but it was vital to the health of the business. It is also paramount in succession planning, and as the business grows, the partners may change through the years.

Wait! You "love" your business, and you "love" your partners. Right?

I spoke to a group of succession planning professionals after selling my business. The group also contained insurance agents, attorneys, financial planners, and even a bereavement counselor. They were curious about how my five-year plan to sell my business worked. I explained I'd spent three years managing the balance sheet and P&L to get them super clean and accurate. It paid off by providing an additional $100,000 in valuation to the business. I then had a two-year marketing plan to actually sell the business. We closed the sale within eighteen months of initiating the plan.

Even though I was the presenter at this meeting, the succession planning group taught me other reasons why you plan for partnership transition at the very same moment you begin the partnership. Here are some of those reasons.

What happens if a partner dies and there are no instructions in their will? The family of the deceased now owns a part of your business. If the family is fighting internally over the will or there is no clear instruction, you have inherited a family of new partners.

What happens if key stakeholders get sick? People have grandchildren in other states. Suddenly, a part-owner wants to move. People get bored. People have sex with people they're not supposed to. People just get mad at each other and have poor coping skills. How does one grow the company? How does one save the company in a downturn? The entrepreneur mindset is usually a bit of a risk-taker, independent, lots of ego type. When difficulties arise or decisions have to be made, strategic processes should have already been set up to deal with issues like sale of the business, retirement of key stakeholders, bankruptcy liabilities, incapacity of decision makers and more. All partners need to agree to these processes in a formal document.

I listened to a succession planning consulting firm detail a case where a family business client was trying to figure out their succession plan. This plan was being forced upon the company because the owner had died unexpectedly. Discussions between the entire family became so contentious the planners had to separate all the stakeholders into different rooms—a parent in one office, each sibling in an office, and each manager/partner in another. It was like an interrogation scene to get the stories from each party separately, then compare the evidence. Sounds like *The Three Stooges*, *The Brady Bunch*, and *Law and Order*, all at the same time!

Don't be that business.

Questions of money do seem to make the Camaro go up on the blocks, and the wheels fall off quicker than anything. The well-being, also known as cash flow, of the business will stay positive when agreed-upon processes are followed. It will also contribute mightily to keeping stress and heart rates at the appropriate level.

Do this for me: Make a vow you'll lay the groundwork for succession or sale of your business from the start, and stay curious and keep learning about what makes your business tick. These elements keep your "marriage to your business" intact and moving toward a "happily ever after"!

Highlights

1. Your business needs and wants your attention. Don't ignore it.
2. Plan for the eventual transitions at the time you start the company.
3. At least once a year, discuss with your partner their feelings, expectations, and plans for the business.
4. Remember to get outside your business on a regular basis for conferences and training. You are not alone!

15

Success vs. Succession Planning

Ricky Bobby's slingshot to the finish line

IN THE PREVIOUS chapter, I mentioned my five-year plan to sell my business. Here, I want to dig a bit deeper into some strategies you might consider when marketing your business and working with employees during the transition. You have to make a judgment call about your situation. Ask (sound familiar?) attorneys, CPAs, bankers, and wealth advisors how similar companies have managed their vendors, customers, and employees during the sale of their business. They have war stories. In our situation, we put a sign on the door: "Franchise for Sale, Owner Retiring." I made sure the employees knew they were being inspected daily by potential new owners and asked them to "stay sharp."

One of the unusual things about the franchise I owned is that ninety percent of resales went to current or former employees and customers. In contrast, when most other businesses go on the market the owners keep it under wraps. They don't want to spook the employees, vendors, or customers. This is probably the best for publicly traded companies due to SEC rules, but for small to medium private companies these employees are a huge part of your saleable asset. Keeping my employees informed and aware of how important they were to the business made the transition a lot less stressful for me—and for my employees.

The reason the franchises' resales drew so many former employees and customers is because people are attracted to success. Employees and customers had witnessed and participated in that success. My success led to an inevitable successful succession.

I think one of the reasons I had success mentoring former employees to own their own businesses, and having some return later as potential buyers of my business, was the process I created for interacting with them from day one. I realized I had empowered my employees to think of themselves as owners during three specific occasions: hiring, evaluation, and real-time feedback.

During the hiring process many small businesses, especially retail, essentially just put out a "help wanted" sign. Thanks to the internet, I no longer search for employees with a sign on the door. (However, it's ironic that's the way I found a new owner.) I never had a "help wanted" sign. Back when I did place a sign on the door it said, "Wanted: conversationalists, problem solvers, talkers!" (In fact, many of my best employees were theater students.) In the interview, I would ask questions aimed at those abilities. Sometime during the conversation, I would let them know I was about their age when I started the company. I would talk about how long they might work there. I would say, "If you are here five years from now, I expect you to be close to buying the place and becoming an owner." It planted the small seed of expectation in their brain at a time when they were really just thinking about a paycheck and a fun place to work.

The second way I planted the seed for a future owner was with scheduled reviews. As mentioned previously, I was a leader in the Boy Scouts. A key part of a youth's transition from one rank to the next was a conversation with a couple of the adult leaders. It is a moment for a young leader that they can converse with adults on a more leader-to-leader level. It is a very empowering conversation. The ranks are earned in this order: Scout, Tenderfoot, Second Class, First Class, Star, Life, and Eagle. When a candidate has earned the rank of "Life" after being a "Star," they are usually about fourteen to sixteen years old. They've been in the unit a while. During the rank transition conference, we'll ask them, "How are things going? What do you like or dislike about our troop? What would you change?" See, at this point the scout knows all the hands-on requirements of being a scout. Sharpening a knife, camping safely, first aid, cooking, etc. Now they are moving on to learning leadership skills. Soft skills. The little folks are looking up to the big folks in the troop. This is a wonderful time to point out that they are a leader. Whether they want to be or not. It is a revelation to them. But here's how we really got their head to explode. We told them they had to start acting like an Eagle Scout—now—long before they've earned the highest and most-honored rank in scouting. Presidents, Nobel Prize recipients, astronauts, scientists, and titans of the business world have all been Eagle Scouts. This scout just received his Life rank and is thinking, "Hey, I can coast for a while." But if you always act like a life scout, you will always be a life scout. Nothing wrong with that. But you don't get the Eagle rank, then start acting like an Eagle. You earn it. You earn it by demonstrating the attitude of an

Eagle now. You look out for jobs that need doing. You anticipate the needs of your unit and fellow scouts. Jump in and ask to help. Do not wait to be asked. Then you are rewarded with the most honored recognition. POW! The light bulbs flash in their brains. Some get it and act on it. Some act on it only for a short while. That is why there are so few Eagles. This is the exact same thing going on in your business. When you explain this concept to an employee, you will see the POW! moment and realization wash across their expression. Many do step up. Want to be an hourly employee forever? Just keep acting like one. An employee gets paid for the job they are doing and, with exception of some cost of living raises, they will continue to earn at that level. The staff member who jumps in without being asked, the one who anticipates the needs of others in the office or team, is the one whose name will come up when a new position or project comes along. This person will be part of your succession plan—and their own success plan!

The third opportunity to encourage ownership-level thinking with an employee happens on the fly during regular operations. So, let me stop and ask—have you watched the movie *Talladega Nights* with Will Ferrell? (If so, go ahead and admit it.) He plays Ricky Bobby in a crazy movie about NASCAR. He and his racing partner win races by pulling off the classic racing maneuver called the slingshot. So how is this done? The lead car has to go as fast as it can, and all the other cars in the pack are chasing it. When the lead car goes that fast, it creates a vacuum right behind it. The trick is for the partner's car to move into the vacuum and draft behind the lead car. At the right moment, the leader will let off a bit, and the partner's car pulls around and is "slingshot" forward with tremendous momentum.

Here's how it works in your business. You've been working hard. Doing lots of everything in your business, then you inform the people or person you want to slingshot: "Hey, I'm going on vacation. I'm going to an out-of-town conference. Don't call me unless the place is on fire. You know more about this business than I did when I started it. Make the decisions. See ya!" Then you leave. You disappear. You create a strategic and planned vacuum in the business. You will return to see a new dynamic. More independence, a bit more walking around with confidence, phone calls with clients handled with more gusto. This is also a key time to make sure you follow up with a good "debriefing" meeting. Ask detailed and pointed questions about the workflow, customer interactions, new business prospects, etc. Too many times I made the mistake of just asking, "So how'd everything go?" The answer was always the same: "Fine." In those situations, I didn't learn anything and neither did the employee who stepped up, nor the employee that DIDN'T step up in my absence.

There are several well-known family-owned businesses that are successful case studies of succession. Walmart, Corning, Chick-fil-A and Cabela's are a few. I believe when you start your business, whether it's a stand-alone or a franchise, you should always keep the endgame in mind. At some point, you will want to get out of the business. Plan on building your asset to be more valuable, every day. And plan your exit.

So, Ricky Bobby—let's go shake and bake!

Highlights

1. Many times, a manager or former employee will buy your business. Place that idea in their head from the beginning of their employment.
2. Even if you don't tell your employees the business is for sale, make sure they know they are always an important asset to the business.
3. Keep giving employees chances to "run the business."
4. Set up a strategic timeline, including the proper management of your balance sheet and P&L, at least three years before beginning the sale process.

EPILOGUE

From thunderbolt to slingshot succession

A FEW DAYS before my dad died, I was sitting in his hospital room, and he asked me, "Is there anything different I could have done with my life?" Before I answered, I thought about his question. The fact is, we make decisions based on the information we have and the emotions affecting us at that exact moment in our lives. I believe if you were to put yourself in an exact moment again, with the same exact amount of information, you would make the same exact decision. And that's what I told him. I hope it gave him a bit of peace.

Out of all the little lessons and tedious information-gathering you will go through as you start and grow your business, the most important thing that brought me through it all was to never lose the drive and purpose given to me in that Thunderbolt moment—the inspirational and confident knowledge that this purpose and this business were right for me. The Thunderbolt got me through the tough times of finding cash and investors to get started. The Thunderbolt got me through the learning curve of the new franchisor's mistakes. The joys of independent business ownership confirmed my Thunderbolt moment, over and over again. Watching the growth in sales, profits, community recognition, and industry acceptance kept recharging my Thunderbolt. It gave me the confidence to understand, even in my despair of growing too fast, that my initial Thunderbolt idea was sound. I just had to get back to it—to reconnect and keep learning. The Thunderbolt gave me energy to ask for help from mentors, when I finally swallowed my pride and learned how important mentors are.

When I maintained the electric Thunderbolt confidence, that energy infused my business even in the toughest of times. My employees stayed motivated, my customers never knew I was struggling, and vendors knew they could count on me to not quit. When the time came to develop a strategic five-year plan to sell my business and slingshot someone else forward into a successful business, there was not a single hiccup. The power never fizzled.

So, no matter where you are on your small business path, whether you are just searching and thinking about it or you are hip-deep in daily tasks of running several locations, I hope my *Scabs, Scars, and Pots o' Gold* brought a smile to your face. I hope you see some things you're doing smarter than me, and perhaps I helped you foresee a pitfall ahead. Either way, if you are reading this book, you've probably got a decision to make. Remember, decisions are the scariest thing in the woods! I know this for certain. Ten years from now, if you never gave owning your own business a try, it will eat at you forever. So gather more information, ask questions, get a mentor, and make a decision! You can do it! I am so glad I did and would do it again! The deep, gut-level satisfaction to have tried and succeeded is what having a life well lived is all about! So grab that Thunderbolt idea tight and go for it!

I want to thank you for reading my book. I am always looking for feedback, questions, and comments, and I'd love to hear from you.

QUESTIONS TO ASK, WISDOM TO GATHER

Questions to Ask or Research about a Potential Franchisor

1. What is the business's history?
2. When did the franchising concept begin or did it start out as a franchise?
3. How many locations?
4. How many company/franchisor-owned locations?
5. What are the territories and how are they determined?
6. Have territory guidelines ever changed?
7. What might cause a territory rules change in the future?
8. How many new stores open each year? Closings? Resales?
9. What are the resale data? Average price? Years owned before resale?
10. What are the demographics of a franchisee owner?
11. What is the franchisor's opinion on changing market conditions as it relates to this concept?
12. What kind of franchisor training? Get the details.
13. What kind of franchisor support and continued training? Get the details.
14. What feedback channels are available for a franchisee?
15. Will the franchisee have a dedicated field operations manager?
16. Are there options for multiple locations and what are the requirements for expansion?
17. Does the franchisor offer financing help?
18. Who are the key vendors?
19. Can franchisees choose their own vendors?
20. What types of marketing expenses are required?
21. What type of marketing support, creatively and in media buying, does the franchisor provide?
22. What future marketing initiatives are on the horizon?
23. Does the franchisor rely on outside vendors for marketing?

24. Do you have a list and contact info of current and past franchisees that I can speak with?
25. What is the resale process?
26. Do you help me with my business plan?
27. What is the typical sales cycle for this concept? Is it regional?
28. What are the upfront costs and continuing royalties? Will they go up?
29. What are typical gross sales, expenses, and how much can I make?
30. How much liquid capital will I need until the business breaks even?
31. How is this franchise concept unique?
32. How much time on-site is required? Do I have to be an owner-operator?
33. Are there locations to work in and/or shadow for a time before deciding?

Questions to Ask a Current or Former Franchisee

1. Is it what you expected? Why or why not?
2. Are you earning what you expected?
3. What do you think of the support and training you are receiving?
4. What did you do before buying your franchise?
5. How many hours a week do you work?
6. Is the marketing support from the franchisor adequate?
7. Is the franchisor accessible?
8. Any other advice?

What All Accountants Should Provide to You

1. Balance sheet
2. Profit and loss
3. Cash flow
4. Tax returns
5. Advice on managing balance sheet to fit the growth goals of the company
6. Advice on company structure before legally forming
7. Advice on possible expense savings/management
8. Advice on accumulating a safety net cash reserve
9. Advice on tax-favorable cash management

ABOUT THE AUTHOR

Scott Ward's experiences as a multi-unit franchisee for over 25 years and mentoring six employees to own their own businesses, gives him a truck load of true-life stories. Scott's unique way of attaching those stories to analogies that stick in one's head is how he came up with the motto, "I tell stories that make businesses money!" Scott is an accomplished speaker and mentor working through groups like SCORE, Toastmasters and the National Speakers Association. A graduate of the University of Florida, School of Journalism & Communications, Scott has worked for a paycheck since he was thirteen. He truly believes in the power of the human spirit and the ability of families to raise up the next generation to higher success. His favorite inspirational song is "Fanfare for the Common Man" by Aaron Copeland.

www.scottbward.net

NOTES

Chapter 1

[1] Jennifer Feldman, "Get to Know the Five Most Popular Preemployment Personality Tests," Top Resume, accessed April 26, 2019, https://www.topresume.com/career-advice/how-to-pass-the-pre-employment-personality-test.

Chapter 2

[1] "Independent Businesses vs Franchises," *Guidant Financial Blog*, last modified August 21, 2018, https://www.guidantfinancial.com/blog/independent-business-ownership-vs-franchising-which-is-right-for-you/

[2] Karsten Strauss, "13 Mistakes New Franchisees Make—And How To Avoid Them," *Forbes*, May 27, 2014, https://www.forbes.com/sites/karstenstrauss/2014/05/27/13-mistakes-new-franchisees-make-and-how-to-avoid-them.

Chapter 4

[1] George Lois, *Damn Good Advice (for people with talent!)* (London: Phaidon Press Limited, 2016), 21.

[2] Observantrambler, "Ted Turner & CNN," *Comm455/History of Journalism*, October 29, 2012, http://historyofjournalism.onmason.com/2012/10/29/ted-turner-cnn/.

[3] "Sir Richard Branson: On A Mission To Mentor," *Motivated Magazine*, May 4, 2011, http://motivatedonline.com/sir-richard-branson-on-a-mission-to-mentor/.

[4] Sirje Virkus, "Henry Ford," *The Concept of Leadership*, Institute of Information Studies, Tallinn University, 2009, https://www.tlu.ee/~sirvir/Leadership/The%20Concept%20of%20Leadership/henry_ford.html.

Chapter 5

[1] The use of the words "X-wing Fighter" and "Star Wars" in no way imply any endorsement by the owners of the trade marks and copy rights. The words "X-Wing fighter" and "Star Wars" are used only as an analogy for educational purposes. These marks are owned exclusively by The Walt Disney Company and Lucas Film Ltd.

[2] See disclaimer comment above

Chapter 6

[1] Greg Dickinson, "CFO Signals," 3Q17 Highlights, Deloitte, October 15, 2017, https://www2.deloitte.com/us/en/pages/finance/articles/cfos-signals-survey-geopolitical-threats-and-political-turmoil-dampen-sentiment.

[2] Laura Petrecca, "Can small firms grow too fast?" *USA Today*, October 21, 2013, https://www.usatoday.com/story/money/business/2013/10/21/smart-small-business-growth/2982391/.

[3] Jayson DeMers, "5 Companies That Grew Too Quickly (and what you can learn from them)," *Entrepreneur Magazine*, March 12, 2018, https://www.entrepreneur.com/article/310166.

Chapter 7

[1] Jennifer Merrill, "Top 25 Mentoring Relationships in History," *The Chronicle of Evidence Based Mentoring*, September 13, 2015,

https://www.evidencebasedmentoring.org/top-25-mentoring-relationships-in-history.

Chapter 8

[1] Ash Ambirge, "Top Nine Ways to Deal with Business Overwhelm (So You Can Avoid Thoughts of Mass Murder)," The Middle Finger Project, October 24, 2011, https://www.themiddlefingerproject.org/?s=top+9+ways.

Chapter 9

[1] Jason G. Goldman, "How Being Watched Changes You—Without You Even Knowing," *BBC Future,* February 9, 2014, https://www.bbc.com/future/article/20140209-being-watched-why-thats-good.

Chapter 10

[1] Justine Hastings and Jesse Shapiro, "Mental Accounting and Consumer Choice: Evidence from Commodity Price Shocks," NBER Working Paper No. 18248, The National Bureau of Economic Research, Cambridge, MA, July 2012, http://www.nber.org/papers/w18248.

[2] Hillary Hoffower, "There are two types of American millennials, says an expert who studies the generation—and the difference between them is not based on their age," *Business Insider,* January 4, 2020, https://www.businessinsider.com/2-types-of-millennials-mega-llennials-and-me-llennials-2020-1.

[3] Natalio Extremera, Sergio Merida-Lopez, Nicolas Sanchez-Alvarez, Cirenia Quintana-Orts, "How Does Emotional Intelligence Make One Feel Better at Work? The Mediational Role of Work Engagement," *The International Journal of Environmental Research and Public Health,* September 2, 2018, https://www.ncbi.nlm.nih.gNov/pmc/articles/PMC6164137/.

Chapter 12

[1] Shawn Achor, Andrew Reece, Gabriella Rosen Kellerman, and Alex Robichaux, "9 Out of 10 People Are Willing to Earn Less Money to Do More-Meaningful Work," *Harvard Business Review*, November 6, 2018.